Conor Cunneen (signature)

WHY IRELAND NEVER INVADED AMERICA

———— ♣ ————

An Insightful, Unique Look at
CORPORATE STRATEGY

———— ♣ ————

Conor Cunneen

SHEIFGAB
Publishing

Published by SHEIFGAB Publishing
1212 S. Naper Blvd
Suite 119-202
Naperville IL 60540
www.sheifgab.com

Design: Wayne E. Johnson
WayneEJ@comcast.net

Proofreading: Gretchen Schlesinger

ISBN 0-9763740-0-5

Printed in the United States of America
First Edition 2005

10 9 8 7 6 5 4 3 2 1

To my beautiful wife, Pat —
the nicest person I've ever met.

To John Paul and Amy

Acknowledgements

Special thanks to Megan O'Connor, Gretchen Schlesinger, Wayne Johnson, Dave Spirk, Paul Schneider, Bob Gluck, Ken Kabira, Tom MacMurray, Naperville Writer's Group and to 'Old Bill' who says he does not want to be mentioned in dispatches, but who has been a fantastic mentor to me both in writing this book and in my speaking career. I would not have been able to funchion (sic) nearly as well without his help.

Contents

Chapter One

Motorway Strategy

— ♣ —

Lesson:
Don't Believe
Your Own Blarney

— ♣ —

" *Gaiety is the most outstanding feature of the Soviet Union.* "

—Joseph Stalin

"Ireland is a warm, welcoming, magical, mystical land—a land of legends and leprechauns. One legend has it, that at the end of every rainbow, you will find a leprechaun and a pot of gold. Leprechauns are fairy-like creatures that bring good luck, well-being and happiness. Locals claim that at dusk, if you are very quiet and very lucky, you might see leprechauns dancing on mushrooms. When Irish people feel upbeat—this is normal—and believe they can achieve anything, it is not unusual to hear them proclaim they could 'dance on mushrooms.' "

Jake Boyd smiled and replaced the airline magazine in the seat pocket in front. If the land of his grandparents was as nice as the many gushing reviews he had read, he would be happy. Already, he could see the green countryside as Aer Lingus flight

129 made its initial approach to touch down at Shannon Airport on the west coast of Ireland.

The prospect of staying with a relative he had never met and previously only communicated with by phone and email was an intriguing one. Just as intriguing was his cousin's name. Finbarr Kozlowski was not the most Irish of names, he mused.

Emotionally and physically exhausted, Jake's thoughts drifted to the need for this seven day vacation. Business had been more difficult in the last year than expected. The seven percent decline in sales was disappointing. Nor could he take pride in the dramatic reduction in margin—a primary contributor to the loss-making year. Jake felt lost and uncertain about the company he founded six years previously.

The recent acquisition proposal from Velt, Frommer-Hell, a venture capital firm, was substantial enough for him to consider selling—something he would not consider if he knew how to rejuvenate what he referred to as his "love child." Jake privately referred to Velt, Frommer-Hell as Vultures from Hell, but he understood the marketplace. If his business could not regain profitability soon, it would die, placing one hundred and seventy employees out of work. The alternative was to accept the Velt, Frommer-Hell proposal.

The gentle bump on landing interrupted his thoughts. The pilot thanked the passengers for their custom and brought a broad smile to Jake's face when he said in a gentle Irish brogue, "You can always be sure of an easy landing here, folks. Our rainy climate ensures we have very soft ground."

Jake collected his bags at the carousel and moved through immigration and customs. He had developed an easy relationship with his cousin during the numerous telephone and internet communications of recent weeks. Finbarr had promised him a welcome he would not forget and was now obviously keeping that promise. Recognizing his cousin from emailed photographs, Jake broke into a laugh. Finbarr Kozlowski was carrying a large placard with the legend 'Jake Boyd go home' written in large strokes. Incongruously, an oversized black cowboy hat with very wide brims rested on his head, partially covering his ears.

"Finbarr?"

"Jake! Welcome to the Emerald Isle, my man. I hope you don't mind the message on this sign. A hundred thousand welcomes to you, man, a hundred thousand welcomes to you." The words were spoken quickly with a light lyrical brogue.

"Thanks for having me. Is this the normal welcome

message you give people, Finbarr?"

"Only to those we like, Cousin, but you know that is nearly everyone."

Finbarr, at twenty-eight, was of a similar age to Jake, but he seemed to carry himself in a lighter, more easy-going manner. The initial introduction and previous communications confirmed Jake's view that his relative had a permanent smile on his face.

"You're traveling pretty light, Cousin," Finbarr said as he loaded the two bags into the trunk of the medium sized sedan.

"I think I've got all I need, including a raincoat, galoshes and umbrella," responded Jake.

"You're generalizing, man. All you'll need for the next week are golf clubs and sun lotion. Oh, and maybe some hangover medicine. Come on, let's move."

Jake moved to the right side of the car until Finbarr reminded him, "Hey, Yank, passengers on the other side. Don't you know we drive on the correct side of the road here?"

The visitor felt uncomfortable sitting in the front left seat, unable to exercise control over the vehicle as Finbarr drove at what seemed terrifying speed on the "correct side of the road."

Jake's anxiety faded as genuine and cordial

conversation developed with his Irish cousin.

Lowering the sound pounding from the car radio, Finbarr said, "So things are pretty tough for you at the moment, business wise? You seemed really down when we spoke on the phone last week. Got to say, you don't convey a lot of optimism in your emails either, Couz. What's the story?"

"I'm tired, Finbarr. I'm tired of the whole entre-preneur thing. Or at least I'm tired of the loss-making entrepreneur thing. I once thought I knew it all and could rule the world. No problem. Now the world is ruling me and I'm close to packing it in. Maybe the world isn't ready for *JB's Good Food* after all."

"That might be true, Couz, but it could be too easy an explanation. Maybe all you need is a bit of fine tuning and you could have a very profitable business. What is your strategy?"

Jake was taken aback by the blunt question and the confidence with which Finbarr was addressing his problem. He did appreciate the genuine concern.

"Finbarr," he took a deep breath, "I'm not sure I know any more. I wanted to introduce a range of gourmet foods under the *JB* brand. Initial reaction was positive with good trade listings, but consumer sales have never been great, and now I'm getting hit with de-listing or threats of de-listings. It seems no matter what we do, business continues to tank."

They were now on a narrow dual lane road, moving far too fast for Jake's comfort. Suddenly Finbarr accelerated and moved the car close to the rear of a large truck. Jake instinctively brought his right foot up to a brake pedal which was not there.

"Whoa, Finbarr, you like tailgating these guys?"

"We'll pull back in a second. Don't worry, Jake. What can you see in front of you?"

"What?"

"What can you see in front of you?"

"How can I see anything in front of me? You've driven so close to this truck that my view is completely obscured," said Jake, his voice rising in concern.

"*That's* what I thought you might say," Finbarr responded. "Think about this, Jake. One of your issues might be you are so close to your problems that you can't really see the wood for the trees anymore. Look what happens when I pull back."

Finbarr slowed the car gently.

"The view gets better. You appreciate your environment better and guess what? You also can react in time when problems occur."

"If only it were that simple, Finbarr, if only..." His voice trailed off—tired.

"Of course, it's not that simple, but you know

strategy is a lot like driving on the road."

"What do you mean?"

"Well, whether you are driving or in business, there's an end objective. Right?"

"Wow, Finbarr, you *are* a genius," Jake said semi-sarcastically.

"Thanks, Couz, I have been called worse, but there is a bit more to it than that."

"Look at how the driving analogy might relate to the business world. Not only do you have an objective in mind, but you also must be able to see what is happening around you. If, as with that truck incident a minute ago, you get too involved, too close, it can impact your ability to see what is really happening."

"Kind of business myopia, you mean."

"That's right. That's right. You know that you need a good understanding and appreciation of your marketplace. Call it market information if you like, but when driving you need the same type of knowledge. Whether on the road or in business, you must be able to read the signs. We're coming up to a nasty cross-road shortly. It's well posted, but most people would not see the sign if stuck tight behind that lorry."

"Behind the what?"

"The lorry—sorry Yankee Couz, I meant the truck.

I'd forgotten you guys don't speak proper English."

"Ha, and you're saying you Irish do. I needed an interpreter to understand what some people were saying back at the airport."

"Don't be getting jealous of the Irish accent now, Couz. We'll have you talking funny by the time you go home."

"Oh, begorah—to be sure, to be sure," said Jake mimicking a Hollywood Irish accent. "The Irish accent would definitely help with the girls, and that's a fact."

"Only over in the States, Jake. Funny thing is your Yankee accent will probably have them swooning here. We might even get you married off—to a red headed Maureen O'Hara type. That'd be a hoot."

"No thanks. I like my freedom. I also like staying alive, so keep back from that truck, will you?"

"Oh, alright. But the point I was trying to make is that you have to pay attention to what is going on around you. If you don't read the signs, you will end up in trouble."

"That's pretty prescient of you, Finbarr."

Finbarr glanced briefly at Jake. "Hey, take it easy there with them big words, Couz. 'Prescient' and 'Myopia.' I can use big words as well, like marmalade and Mercedes-Benz you know," he said, breaking into a laugh.

"Seriously, Jake, let me explain. We're driving now at seventy miles per hour."

"I know, and the speed limit is fifty-five, or did you not see the signs you have been preaching about?"

"I saw it, but that is only one part of knowing your market. Not only do you need to read the signs, but you must also rely on experience. I drive this road a few times a week and have rarely seen a speed trap, so I reckon I'm pretty safe here. Sure, I'm taking a risk, but one that is realistic based on my knowledge of my environment."

Finbarr gestured to his rear view mirror.

"Jake, I've been looking in my mirror for a while. We have a Michael Schumacher type-of-guy weaving in and out of traffic trying to get to somewhere real fast."

Even as Finbarr was finishing his sentence, a red sub-compact overtook them at a speed which surprised Jake.

"Oh my Gawd, what speed is that lunatic doing?"

"Eighty five—ninety maybe. That guy is like your competition, Jake. He is taking a lot of risks to get to his objective faster than others."

"Yeah, if he's looking to go to heaven or hell."

"Let's hope that doesn't happen. He might go off

the road at some stage, but he may not. Most drivers or companies who move that fast and take that many risks will run into difficulty, but some will survive. Those are the ones that businesses have to worry about."

"Hey, Finbarr, be careful. You are being prescient again, and what's even more worrying—you are making sense."

"Why thank you, Cousin, you can repay me later when we stop for a bevy."

"A bevy? That's some form of liquid refreshment, is it?"

"You got it, man; I told you we'd have you speaking funny before you left."

"*Now*, look at what's ahead of us," said Finbarr in an exasperated tone, as he slowed aggressively to avoid hitting a large black sedan hogging the fast lane.

"This is just one further illustration of how companies behave. The driver in front has no idea I am behind him. That guy is as happy as Farmer Brown's pig at a trough, just ambling along with not a care in the world. Not, of course, that pigs amble along when at a trough, but you know what I mean. There are a lot of companies out there, Jake, hogging their lane. Organizations that think they know it all and have nothing to worry about, and then suddenly —BOOM—they're hit by the iceberg, if you don't mind me mixing my road and sea metaphors. Some organizations are really slow to read the signs. Life-affecting changes have to be spelled out for them, and they're still slow to react. I think there's a song that goes '*When You Wrapped My Lunch in a Road Map, I Knew You Meant Good-Bye,*' which sums up just how much notice some companies require to be able to see their reality."

Jake looked at Finbarr in amused astonishment.

"That's one way of putting it. I guess there are a few companies out there who are fat, dumb and happy."

"More than a few. A lot more. Did you ever get listed by Kmart?"

Jake was surprised at Finbarr's question, but then recalled his email to Finbarr, outlining some of the business problems.

"Nope. Never did. We thought we might get limited distribution but it never happened, and in any event Kmart—hey, hold on a minute—I see what you mean, Kmart got hit by the iceberg," said a now animated Jake.

"Welcome to the real world, Jake. Kmart sure did hit an iceberg and they were icons of retailing at one stage.

"I got a copy of *In Search of Excellence* from the

library a few weeks back."

"The Peters and Waterman book?"

"That's the one. It's not new but it's still a great read. Most of what's in it makes a lot of sense, but what I found really interesting is the number of companies cited as being excellent in that book, which eventually sank faster than the Titanic."

"Was Kmart cited as an excellent company?"

"Yup. In fact according to the authors, it passed all the hurdles for excellent performance in the twenty years preceding the study. Mind you, there were quite a few other companies mentioned that haven't made it. At least Kmart has survived—what do you call it—Chapter Eleven, yeah?"

"Yes, that's right. And now they are merging with Sears. Who else was cited in the book?"

"Can't remember all of them now, but others that fell into that twenty-year window of excellence included Digital Equipment or DEC as it became known before its demise, Eastman Kodak and Polaroid, would you believe?"

"Finbarr, those guys are virtual basket cases now. What happened?"

"I don't know for sure, but I reckon they were a little like our friend in the car in front who thinks he is doing a good job—he is going somewhere—but really has no idea what is going on around him. Companies are like people, Jake. They get complacent and sometimes that can be fatal. Hopefully, our friend ahead doesn't have that problem, although I tell you if he doesn't move his butt out of my way soon, I'll stop being a nice friendly Irishman and, Cousin, you'll see a different side of me.

"*Ah, I don't believe it,*" Finbarr said in an exasperated manner. "No—I *do* believe it."

"Believe what? What are you talking about?" queried Jake.

"This guy in front. Look at him; he's braking, turning left and no indicator. But I shouldn't be surprised, and you know what Jake—*that,*" he said, gesturing to the driver who was now moving left, "*that* is just the way some organizations operate today. They change direction or strategy without ever giving notice to stakeholders or employees. It's no wonder some companies fail."

Jake slowly became more comfortable with Finbarr's driving. His growing comfort level allowed for appreciation of the green Irish countryside, while remaining intrigued at the logical manner by which his cousin approached problems.

"Hey Finbarr, is that our friend in the red car there?"

Finbarr looked at the red sub-compact which had

overtaken them some time ago. It was now pulled to the side of the road where a police officer appeared to be writing a ticket.

"I think it is. He's obviously been done for speeding. I've never seen a speed trap here before, but that just reinforces what I said earlier. Sometimes you win when you take risks, sometimes not. That driver might try the same thing again tomorrow and he may well get to his destination faster than you or I would. Those are the guys you have to worry about in business. You know, Jake, maybe you should be one of those guys who moves fast, takes risks and gets there faster than the big guys."

"Don't disagree, but you know something, Mr. Know-it-all, you've just fallen into the trap you've been talking about. If that guy hadn't been pulled for speeding, you probably would have. You were complacent about your environment and it could have cost you."

Finbarr thought for a moment. "Hmm. I think I'm going to have to use the 'P' word, Jake. Prescient. That indeed is very prescient of you. Very PP indeed."

"Well, at least it shut you up for a minute, but it makes you wonder how you, me, companies in general can avoid complacency. I mean everyone believes their own blarney. But, it does make me think I should spend more time on what you might call motorway strategy. I think I have been too close to the 'lorry' in front to use your analogy. I think I have also spent too much time looking in my rear view mirror, wondering what happened and not really learning from it. For a time, we had been making adequate profit and I was happy with that. Content to do what we had always done."

Jake paused for a moment, then commented,

"Jeez, Finbarr, maybe I was a bit like that car you said was hogging the road—oblivious to everything going on around."

Finbarr tapped his fingers to the music from the car radio. He cleared his throat, as if hesitating and said, "Jake, I don't mean to beat you up too much— this is meant to be a holiday for you, but have you worked through your company strengths and weaknesses recently?"

Now Jake swallowed a little uncomfortably. "Well, we think about them, but we're just so busy firefighting that it's difficult."

"Sure it is, but let me tell you a little story. The story goes that an Irish general and a U.S. general met at a military conference. Let's call them General Paddy and—what'd be a good name for a U.S. top brass guy—let's call him Hank. Yeah, I like that, Hank—General Hank IV. Anyway, one night over a few drinks, they start joshing each other about the strengths of their respective armies."

"I didn't even know you Irish had an army, Finbarr."

"It's a small one, Jake, but shut up with your Yankee one-upmanship and let me continue. Hank IV commented that the U.S. military could invade and conquer Ireland within a few hours. General Paddy took umbrage at the comment. 'Don't be daft, you could not. Don't you know that as soon as you invaded, you'd be seduced by the charm and loquaciousness of the Irish? We'd persuade you to lay down your arms within a few hours.'

"IV replied, 'That's a load of hogwash, Paddy, and you know it. Even if there were some truth in that, we'd provide our troops with audio devices to prevent them listening to all the blarney you guys go on with.'

"Paddy responded, 'Maybe you would Hank, maybe you would. But what would your troops do when they become enchanted with the beauty of our Irish colleens, who have bewitched every foreigner to our fair land, and, by the way, bewitched, bothered and bewildered every poor Irish male at the same time. And Hank, you couldn't escape their beauty even at night time, because you high-tech guys have them new fangled night goggle thingy-things now.'

"This type of banter went on for a few minutes between General Paddy and IV, with Hank unable to convince Paddy that an invasion would be easy. Eventually, in frustration, General Hank the Fourth said, 'Paddy, if you guys are so good, how come you don't invade America?'

"General Paddy hesitated for a moment, looked General Hank in the eye and said, 'That's easy, Hank. If we did, how would we feed all the prisoners?' "

When Jake finally finished laughing, he turned to his cousin, "Nice story, Finbarr, but what's the point?"

"I'll tell you what the point is, Jake. You have to know your strengths and you have to know your weaknesses. Just having a good idea is not sufficient to be successful. You need to know what markets to attack and what markets not to attack. And you're not going to find that information unless you actively look for it and are *not* seduced by your environment."

"And don't believe your own blarney. Right, Finbarr?"

"That's right. That's right," said a contrite, smiling Finbarr. "And don't believe your own blarney."

Jake smiled with Finbarr. He also thought this

seven day vacation might be much more interesting than expected.

Chapter Two

My Prize Bull

─────────── ♣ ───────────

Lesson:
Vision

─────────── ♣ ───────────

We set out to educate our customers about the romance of coffee drinking.

—Howard Schultz,
Starbucks

"**J**ake, Jake, get out of that bed, you lazy sod. Breakfast is ready in five minutes."

He climbed slowly out of bed and got his bearings. Despite the time difference, Jake had slept well and vaguely appreciated Finbarr's Irish brogue haranguing him about breakfast.

Quickly showering and dressing, he walked into the kitchen where Finbarr was engrossed at a laptop computer.

"Morning, Yank, how'd you sleep?"

"I crashed, Finbarr. I needed a good rest."

"That's good. You left me talking to myself for the last thirty minutes of the drive last night. You really did look whacked. Now, what do you want for breakfast?"

"I thought you said it was ready!"

"I did, but that was only foreplay. Whettin' your appetite like. I'm having coffee and Special K. I've also got some of that wimp coffee—the decaffeinated stuff, if you'd like that."

"Coffee and toast will do fine. Where's the big Irish breakfast I keep reading about? I was expecting bacon, eggs, mushrooms, hash browns and what do you call it, blood pudding?"

"Sure, like you have pancakes every morning back in the States. And by the way, we call it black pudding. You've been reading too many tourist articles, Jake."

"I guess I have. Some things are a bit different here to what I expected. I was glad you didn't ask me to go for a pint of Guinness last night. Back home, they told me we'd be in the pub every night."

"Naw, no point. If you're going to get religion, you might as well stay awake, at least. You'd have fallen asleep and drowned in your Guinness last night," said Finbarr, an impish grin lighting his face.

Jake looked out the kitchen window at a view that was just as he imagined it might be. The airline magazine was correct. Ireland *is* a warm, magical, mystical land. Green fields bordered by dew-dropped rough hedgerows glistened in the morning sun. In the distance, rolling hills were littered with dots of wool—hundreds of sheep. A light mist covered the higher points like a blanket.

"This is some view you have here, Finbarr. You've done well."

"Thanks. I like it. On a clear day, I can see for miles. Nothin' to obstruct my vision."

Jake thought back to the previous day's conversation. "Different to my vision—my business vision, I mean, which is a bit like the top of that mountain— foggy."

"Stop beating yourself up. Your problem is you haven't taken time to appreciate the view. As a result you're unsure of your footing. That's metaphorically speaking if you know what I mean like." Finbarr's ability to speak swiftly, without hesitation sometimes slowed Jake's comprehension.

"... Oh, I see what you mean. Go on, kick a man when he's down."

"No need to get upset, Yank, but I did some work here ..." Finbarr pointed to the computer, "... on corporate vision and your situation in particular." He pushed his chair back from the table where the computer rested. "I want to ask you a question, Jake."

Jake looked quizzically at Finbarr and sipped from the coffee he had poured. "Uh, uh! Sounds very serious for this hour of the morning. Go on, hit me."

"If you were to ask your employees to outline the company vision, do you think they could?"

Jake thought for a moment. "Finbarr, that is one very good question. And I'm not sure I can give a good answer."

"Do you think that might be part of your problem?"

Jake shifted uneasily. This reminded him of a school class, where the teacher asked the question to which you should, but did not, have the answer.

"Finbarr, I'm just trying to sell some product. Vision seemed a great concept in business school. The real world is different—not because I don't believe in vision, but there are other more urgent things to deal with. Every single day."

"There's an old adage, Jake, 'Having lost sight of our objective'..."

"Yeah, yeah, I know—'we redoubled our efforts.' "

"That your situation, Jake?"

"Well, I guess we sometimes do run around like headless chickens. It's difficult to have a vision when you are headless."

"Can't argue with that. Don't worry. It'll happen. Look, I don't know your market that well, but some of the things you are doing do not appear to be completely aligned."

"What do you mean?"

With a twinkle in his eye, Finbarr responded, "Well, by aligned I mean ..."

An irritated Jake interrupted, "I know what aligned means, you dumb Irish Mick, you. What are you trying to tell me?"

"Jake, you sell gourmet foods, yet last night you indicated Kmart was a target customer for you. Is that the right place to sell gourmet food? I'm just askin'. Don't take offense, now. Here's another thing.

"Your brand name, Jake, *JB's Good Food*. It's kinda weird."

"Jeez, you do wonders for a person's confidence."

"Well, maybe 'weird' is the wrong word. But *JB's Good Food* conveys 'healthy' and 'wholesome' to this 'dumb Mick.'"

"Finbarr, I was wrong. Whatever you are, you are not dumb. A pain in the butt, maybe, but dumb—no way. I mean, you *never* shut up. To be fair to you, you're not the first person that has made that point about the '*Good Food*' name."

Jake paused for a moment and wondered if he should ask for further advice. Finbarr kept stating the blindingly obvious, but always it seemed with an interesting twist. Jake proceeded. "O.K., Finbarr, let's assume you and me wished to create a clear vision:

How would we do it?"

"That's the million euro question, Jake. I say that by the way, because the euro is worth a lot more than your greenback. And who would have thought that a few years ago?"

"The worm will turn, my Irish cousin. Now stop thrashing Alan Greenspan and give me the Irish version of vision."

"Well, she'd be a redhead, lovely long legs, great pair of ..."

"Finbarr, are you on drugs or what?"

"... eyes. No need for drugs man. Life's too good. Right! Vision. Simple to talk about, difficult to create, and well nigh impossible to drive effectively through many organizations. But if you get it right, if you have the right vision, it can really energize the workforce. Look at that new airline you've got over in the East Coast. The Bluejet crowd."

Jake hesitated, confused. "You mean JetBlue, don't you," happy he was able to correct Finbarr.

"That's right. That's right. But I reckon Bluejet is a better name because they sure are giving some of them big airlines the blues. Muddy Waters could have done a good blues number for those guys that are gettin' their ass whipped."

Finbarr started singing in an exaggerated blues

style, eyes closed, while playing an imaginary guitar.

"*I got them bad, the bad jet blues*
I can't make no money
Cos to give 'em their dues
JetBlue—they sure took my honey.
Yea, I got them bad, the bad, bad, bad—
bad jet blues."

Jake winced good-humoredly. "That was reminiscent of some of the great blues singers, Finbarr."

"I did think it was creative myself—kind of a cross between Robert Johnson and Leadbelly."

"That's what I mean. Those guys are dead—just like your song."

"Yank, you don't appreciate quality. That is your problem."

Finbarr then slapped the table enthusiastically, grinning broadly and obviously happy with himself.

"You know what, Jake, I am a genius."

"As long as you believe it, Finbarr."

"I just realized—they should actually call the airline Blue and RedJet. Not only is it giving the big airlines the blues, it is also forcing them into the red. Now what do you think about that, Yank?"

"This Yank thinks your brain is too active this hour of the morning, Finbarr... Please," Jake said in an imploring tone, "*please* tell me, you're not going to sing another song."

"You know what? You're just like those record execs that refused to sign The Beatles."

"Hope I'm not that blind, but they didn't have much vision, Finbarr. We can both agree on that."

"That's right. That's right. But let's get serious here for a minute. Bluejet—O.K., O.K., I'm going to be serious. JetBlue has a very clear vision. Do you know what their head honcho, David Neeleman, said when he founded the airline? The objective is to bring 'humanity back to air travel.' Make a profit as well of course."

"They're certainly doing that." Jake nodded in agreement.

"And you know why? Because everything they do is geared towards the vision—bringing humanity back to air travel. JetBlue hires staff, they are called crewmembers, who will live that vision. JetBlue trains people to live that vision and then expects each member to reinforce it amongst others.

"And you know what else the vision does for the airline? It defines the product offered, which in many ways is better than the product offered by the large full-service airlines," said Finbarr.

"Yeah, apparently it provides leather seating and TV monitor for every passenger. United and

American don't do that."

"That's right. That's right. JetBlue offers twenty-four satellite channels at no charge. Think about it, Jake. The vision to bring humanity back to air travel results in customers receiving a better experience at much lower cost than they receive from the big guys—the so called full-service airlines."

"You've got a point there, Finbarr. I do know JetBlue tops the customer satisfaction ratings among U.S. airlines. And it's all because of vision, you say."

"No, you daft git. It is not *all* because of vision, but the vision has helped the airline create an environment to satisfy customers better than its competitors."

"Finbarr, you'll enjoy this JetBlue story, and it reinforces what you're saying.—Some guy who was traveling JetBlue went to the restroom during a flight. While he was, shall we say 'engaged in his business,' there was a knock on the door and a voice said—'Don't forget to use the hand-towels, young man, they are over the wash basin.' This voice was actually a mother who was making sure that her little darling did the right thing, but she tapped on the wrong door. However, our intrepid traveler who got the advice went back to his seat and said to his wife, 'I know JetBlue is big into customer service, but staff telling you where the hand towels are when you are sitting on the throne is above and beyond.'"

Finbarr smiled. "Nice one, Jake. It's probably a BS story but isn't it amazing how fast a legend can grow? Sometimes it's good, sometimes not. But whatever way you look at it, JetBlue seems to be living its vision and getting kudos as a result. 'Tis an amazin' performance."

"You guys have Ryanair over here. I hear they run the same kind of airline and pretty successfully too. Right?"

"Yes and no. Ryanair and JetBlue both claim to be low fare airlines. Both are profitable, but there is divergence from that point. Ryanair would probably laugh at bringing humanity back to air travel. The Ryanair vision is to be *the* low cost European airline and nothing, Jake, *nothing* gets in the way of that mission. Some of Ryanair's competitors think Michael O'Leary—the Ryanair head guy—is a few seats short of the full airplane himself, but that's because he is so fanatic about achieving the Ryanair vision. To ensure that Ryanair is the low cost airline, it flies to out-of-the-way regional airports..."

Southwest Airlines, thought Jake.

"... thus incurring very low landing fees. It has only one airplane type—737s, to keep maintenance, training and other costs down," Finbarr continued.

Jake interjected, "JetBlue has the same policy on planes, although they use Airbus, I think."

"That's right. That's right. But it is moving away from one plane type. JetBlue will soon take a large order of planes from Embraer."

"The Brazilian company?"

"That's right. That's right. Embraer manufactures smaller planes. Hundred-seater, something like that. Introducing those planes might mean JetBlue will be adding complexity and cost to their system. But, on the other hand, the new aircraft will allow them to operate to smaller markets—many of which have never experienced humanity in air travel. But to get back to 'Mighty Mick O'Leary' and Ryanair, the airline does not have designated seating. Why? Because it slows boarding and Ryanair has this 'revolutionary' view that planes don't make money on the ground."

Southwest, thought Jake.

"Turnaround time is scheduled at an amazing twenty-five minutes. That's from the time the plane arrives at the gate, to closing the plane door for departure. All of those factors have ensured that Ryanair is the most profitable airline in Europe. And get this, Jake, 'Might Mick' now says Ryanair will remove seat pockets because they take up space and are time consuming to clean."

Jake nodded. "In other words, they add cost, but provide no great function."

"That's right. That's right. He is also getting rid of reclining seats due to high maintenance costs. The vision to be the low cost airline is driving everything that company does. If you want anything on board— drinks, food, anything—you are charged for it."

"It's the Southwest model, Finbarr. In fact, I think Ryanair studied Southwest."

"I'm not boring you with this stuff, am I?"

"No way. You see, I know all this stuff or something similar. I might just take a leaf out of Richard Nixon's book."

"Who?—'Tricky Dicky'? What can he teach you?"

"Nothing about bugging buildings, that's for sure. Nixon said the most creative period of his life occurred after he left the White House—when he had time to reflect and think. This was never my plan for this vacation, but maybe I can use it as a creative period, time to reflect and think and maybe listen to some of your goofball logic."

"Good job. I'm not sensitive. You sure I won't bore you?"

Pouring another cup of coffee, Jake said, "I'll risk

it. Indeed, I'll challenge you—let's try and develop a vision together."

"Hey, that'd be fun. I'm sure some marketing gurus will disagree with me here, Jake, but creating a corporate vision might be the easiest part of the exercise. You must decide what it is you want your staff and your customers, to think, to know, and to feel about your business. You've got to say, 'This is what I want my customers to think about my business or brand after they have experienced it.' "

"Agree with you, Finbarr. Although, I'm not sure I should try and develop a vision on my own. Maybe I should discuss it with some of my team when I go back."

"Mightn't be a bad idea, but I guess you already have a pretty good idea what you want your customers to be saying about your brand."

"I do. I'd like them to say, 'I can't live without *JB*'s great products,' but I don't think they are saying that. Let me think about this for a while. Do you believe every organization should have a vision?"

"Probably, Jake. It doesn't matter what product or service you offer, employees can benefit from it and ultimately customers. But it is a lot more than words though. I mean you can create a vision that seems logical for any organization, but it doesn't necessarily make sense."

"Cousin, you're losing me."

"Well, let's look at some place like Mountjoy Jail. That's our version of San Quentin Prison. What do you think their vision or mission statement might be?"

"I dunno. Maybe 'Great Bed and Breakfast.'" Jake laughed, impressed at his levity.

"Not bad, Yank, but I've got a better one. Could you imagine the new inmate to San Quentin, reading ..."

"That's if he can read, Finbarr."

"That's right. That's right. But can you imagine him reading a vision or mission statement that goes something like:

'Here in San Quentin, We are dedicated to your security.

Here in San Quentin, Your freedom is our number one concern.'

"On one hand, Jake, it makes sense, but of course it's a load of horse manure. And that is the problem with so many vision and mission statements. Great words. Great message, but no belief in them. And no genuine effort to follow through."

"It's strange though, Finbarr. Some organizations seem to survive even stupid visions. When Henry Ford said, 'You can have any color car you like, as long as it is black,' that was not customer friendly, yet

Ford has thrived, or at least continued to be successful."

"Jake, to some extent, Old Man Ford got a bad rap."

Finbarr was again scanning his computer, as if looking for something. "Sure he did live by that 'Any color as long as it is black' mantra for a time. Nearly died by it as well. The guy had to close his plants to re-tool in 1927. The Ford Motor Company lost brand leadership because of that philosophy."

"And has never regained it back in the States. So why are you saying he got a bum rap?" said Jake, probingly.

"Remember, I said I had been doing some thinking on vision. I keep notes on business matters here." Finbarr beckoned Jake to the computer. "Look at what Ford said was his vision:

'I will build a motor car for the multitude. It shall be large enough for the family, but small enough for the unskilled individual to operate more easily and care for and it shall be light in weight that it may be economical in maintenance ... It shall be so low in price that the man of moderate means may own one and enjoy with his family the blessings of happy hours spent in God's great open spaces.'

"Ford knew what he wanted to do and everything he did was geared to achieving that vision. The end result, Jake—fifteen million Model T's."

"I never thought of Henry Ford as a visionary, Finbarr. I had this perception of an old crotchety guy who never listened to the customer, but when I think about it—you might already know this, wise-guy, he did one other thing which was outlandish at the time, yet probably resulted in greater sales volume. Ford was the first major industrialist to offer a wage of five dollars per day. That was double what other manu-facturers were paying.

"I thought his original logic was to reduce the incredible level of absenteeism, but when you take it in the context of that vision statement you just men-tioned..."

"That's right. That's right. Ford's logic was, he wanted the working man to afford his cars, but he was also clear sighted enough to know, as you said, that if he offered a decent wage, absenteeism would fall. Of course, productivity increased as a result, prices fell, and more people could afford his cars."

"Old Man Ford knew what he was doing alright," said Jake.

"That's right. That's right. The price of the Model T eventually fell from an initial eight hundred and fifty dollars to two hundred and sixty." Finbarr's attention moved back to the computer screen. "Here, look at what Walt Disney's vision was. This was in his investor proposal *before*, Jake, *before* he ever built any of his theme parks:

'*The idea of Disney is a simple one. It will be a place for people to find happiness and knowledge. It will be a place for parents and children to share pleasant times in one another's company: a place for teachers and pupils to discover greater ways of understanding and education. Here the older generation can recapture the nostalgia of older days gone by and the younger generation can savor the challenge of the future.*'

"The amazing thing about this vision is that it is still so apt, more than half a century later. Sure, Disney has had its ups and downs, but there has never been any doubt about what it wants to achieve, and in general, has achieved it."

"You've really got me thinking now, Finbarr. My favorite example of 'vision' is the John F. Kennedy one, about putting a man on the moon by the end of the decade."

"That *was* a great vision, Jake. Many of Kennedy's advisors told him, it couldn't be done— land a man on the moon by the end of the decade, but he went ahead and made the commitment.

"Kennedy's vision statement shows the importance of creating the right vision for the time. Look at the recent statement by George W. Bush about a manned flight to Mars. That is a huge undertaking—probably even more audacious than putting a man on the moon, but no one seems to be even slightly interested in it."

"Good point. So what's the difference, Finbarr?"

"You've got to have the right vision for your time, Jake. When Kennedy made his statement about putting a man on the moon, your country was actually behind the USSR in the space race, the Bay of Pigs debacle had occurred, and the Cold War was heating up big time. You know, I've often wondered how a Cold War heats up. But anyway, Kennedy wanted a vision that would energize the U.S. and help it regain confidence it itself. The vision of 'landing a man on the moon, and returning him to earth safely,' was spot on for those times. Today, the U.S. doesn't need to prove its superiority to anyone, and funding a mission to Mars will not help in its battle with today's biggest enemy—terrorism."

"What you're saying is, a vision should be relevant."

"That's right. That's right. Kennedy's moon vision is a great example and one that was ultimately achieved. Jake, do you wanna see my fave example of a vision?"

"Do I have a choice?"

"No."

Finbarr scanned his computer, double clicking the mouse a number of times.

"This is recounted by Joe Califano in his book *The Triumph and Tragedy of Lyndon Johnson*. It's a bit crude, Jake, and the language could not be used in corporate-land, but this is a great example of making it very clear what someone wishes to achieve. What do you think?"

Jake read with growing astonishment the copy on the computer screen.

"Johnson wanted to pull a conference together on civil rights in 1966. When his advisors asked him what kind of a conference he wanted, this is what he replied:

'In the hill country in the spring, the sun comes up earlier and the ground gets warmer, and you can see the steam rising and the sap dripping. And in his pen, you can see my prize bull. He's the biggest best hung bull in the country. In the spring he gets a hankering for those cows, and he starts pawing the ground and getting restless. So I open the pen and he goes down the hill, looking for a cow, with his pecker hanging hard and swinging. Those cows get so goddamned excited, they get more and more moist to receive him, and their asses just start quivering

and then they start to quiver all over, every one of them is quivering, as that bull struts into their pasture.

'Well, I want a quivering conference. That's the kind of conference I want. I want every damn delegate quivering with excitement and anticipation about the future of civil rights and their future opportunities in this country.'"

"Finbarr, that man had a way with words. I doubt I'll use that language in my vision, but I guess everyone knew what Johnson's vision for the conference was. You can over-promise when it comes to vision though."

"Tell me."

"Well, there is one anecdote about Winston Churchill—arguably one of the greatest visionaries of all time."

"Well, he was definitely PP when it came to Hitler, and also the Iron Curtain."

"Dat's right. Dat's right," said Jake, mocking Finbarr's mannerism. "Churchill owned a successful race-horse, which lost a race late in its career. Churchill was asked to explain. His response was, 'I told the horse if he won, he could spend the rest of his life in stud. The trouble was—the horse couldn't keep his mind on the race.' Now isn't that as good a piece of blarney as any you've told me."

"That it is, Jake. That it is. And a good point made

at the same time," he said, slapping him playfully on the back.

"O.K., Finbarr. Let's recap. You believe a vision should be relevant. People should believe in it, buy in to it, and it should energize the organization. I have two choices in terms of creating my corporate vision. I can create it myself or develop it with my business colleagues. Right?"

"Right. It is your company, your money, your idea, but at the same time it is not just your livelihood that is involved here. Maybe that is the balance you should strike in developing your new company vision."

"O.K., so I set the core vision, but leave it open for improvement or enhancement. When I do develop one, I should live it and breathe it. That way, other people will live it and breathe it as well." Jake nodded in a satisfied manner.

"Remember what you said, Jake. Live it and breathe it. Live it and breathe it. Now, let's work on a short-term and a long-term vision."

Jake sighed, shook his head. "Finbarr, this is great stuff, but let's take a break and come back to this later."

"You're reading my mind, Jake. The short-term vision is we go to the golf course and whack the little round ball. The long-term vision is just as important and my long term vision is that once we finish that game of golf we park ourselves over in Jack McCarthy's Bar and get us some religion—a beautiful pint of Guinness."

"Now, Finbarr, *that* is a vision I can relate to. Let's go."

Chapter Three

Beer For My Horses

--- ♣ ---

Lesson:
The Brand Name

--- ♣ ---

We're more popular than Jesus now.

—John Lennon

Jake had not played a round of golf in a year, but, a natural athlete, he soon rediscovered his passion for the game and his golf swing. Finbarr, who claimed to be an 'enthusiastic bad golfer' was an accomplished player. He did not let Jake forget the recent conversation they had on vision.

On the few occasions Jake failed to connect sweetly with the golf ball, Finbarr commented, "Yank, you're interfering with our vision. Hit fewer bad shots and we'll be down in Jack McCarthy's Bar a lot faster. Not only are you delaying our vision, you are screwing Guinness sales. That's a mortal sin, you know. Jack McCarthy's Bar will go out of business if we don't get there soon, man."

Finbarr landed in trouble as often, but had an appropriate response to each comment Jake threw at him. Following one particularly poor shot, Jake could not resist haranguing Finbarr. "Come on, Irish, the pub will be sold out by the time you finish up. Keep that long-term vision in mind, will you?"

"Yank, life and strategy are a journey. They don't always go smoothly. Just you remember as you work on your vision and implement it, there's going to be a few times when you too end in the rough or in the bunker."

"Finbarr, you are so full of BS, it's amazing you are able to walk."

"Jake, flattery will get you far. Indeed, I'll let you buy the first pint after I've whipped your butt on this golf course."

Jack McCarthy's Bar proved to be a welcome oasis following the golf game. The white walls and thatched roof of the bar whispered 'Welcome' to Jake.

Finbarr was well known to the barman. "Howz it go-ann, Finbarr? You been out gettin' a bit of the sun, I see."

"Sure have, Pat. I was playing the Ryder Cup here with Jake, my Yankee cousin. I think we agreed to share the trophy for another year. Now, pull us two fine pints there, please, because my cousin is parched and I don't think he should drink on his own. Can't have him getting into bad habits when only visiting for a few days."

"Coming up, Finbarr, coming up."

Sitting at the bar, Jake scanned the interior of the pub. Walls were covered with framed photographs of sporting occasions; many were sports Jake had difficulty comprehending. Sports jerseys bearing the logo, "Jack McCarthy's Bar," bedecked the far wall.

"Finbarr, a person could die of thirst here. How long does it take to pour a pint of Guinness?"

"Jake, you are a heathen. Do you not know that Guinness is a religious experience, man? It is also a cultural experience and a work of art. You cannot, Jake, you cannot rush a work of art, no matter how much you want to. Can you imagine how da Vinci would have felt, when painting the Mona Lisa, like, if he got a phone call from his patron to say, 'Hey, Leo, is da painting of me missus ready yet?' He wouldn't have been too impressed, me lad, not too impressed at all. It's the same with this black magic we are waiting on. Guinness isn't just a product. It is an experience, and that, me boyo, is what you should be offering your customers with your products—an experience. You've got to give them a reason to purchase beyond just the core product."

Two pints of Guinness appeared in front of the

cousins. Jake moved to lift his pint and was gently chided by Finbarr.

"Take it easy, man. Just look at that work of art in front of you. Appreciate it. Don't drink it yet, it hasn't settled. Look. Look and wonder at the way those tiny orphan bubbles are moving through the glass, seeking rest in some Guinness wonderland. When those bubbles finally cease, when those brown clouds finally settle, when you have a clean black beautiful pint in front of you, that—Jake, that, is when you raise the magical brew to those parched lips of yours."

"Jeez, you're making this like a sacred experience."

"And is it not?" said Finbarr, his voice rising in mock horror. "You know, we have numerous Guinness connoisseurs who come in here every night, not for the drink mind, but just to be able to watch—and wonder—and wait, as their pint of Guinness settles."

"Yeah, right. Of course, to appreciate that a few times a night, they have to drink the pint."

"That's right. That's right. But that's only an after-thought, a side benefit, like. I reckon those guys would rather watch the pint settle than look at Pamela Anderson."

"They're obviously perverts, Finbarr. Now do you

mind if I take my first drink?"

"Knock it back, Jake. You deserve it. But when doing it, remember, that it's more than the product you are consuming."

Jake sipped at the creamy pint and wiped his upper lip in appreciation.

"It's like mother's milk, isn't it, Jake?"

"Yeah, it's good stuff. Guinness must be one of the best known brands in the world, Finbarr."

"That's right. That's right. You know you can debate until the cows come home how Guinness developed the image and loyalty it has today, but whatever it is, Guinness and a small number of other brands have a unique magic which ensures that their consumer pull—brand loyalty if you like—is much greater than it logically should be. A kind of 'je ne sais quoi' if you will."

"Ooh, that's pretty posh."

"Shut up and drink your pint. I'm trying to be serious here. You can't put a value on that brand magic. It's what Harley-Davidson has got and it's what Starbucks has got. Jake, if you could ever develop a sense of magic around your brand, that is when you will start to make some real money, because consumers will be buying your product—not for its core, but for something intangible."

"I have thought about that, Finbarr. I ride a Harley-Davidson Road King back home. Guess what?"

"Wha?"

"I paid about five grand more for that machine than a comparable one from a Japanese manufacturer. In my heart of hearts, I know the Harley is not worth the premium in terms of pure product quality or reliability. It's a great bike, but so is the competition. Like you say, I was buying something intangible when I got the Harley. It is irrational, it is illogical and yet, I'm like millions of others who fall for that brand magic you're talking about. What's the secret, wise-guy?"

"Now, Jake, if I knew that, do you think I'd be still here, owning just this pub and the petrol—sorry, Yank, gas—station down the road?"

Jake looked at Finbarr in astonishment.

"I never knew you owned this pub. You're a sly dog alright. But what's with the name. How come Kozlowski owns a place called 'Jack McCarthy's?'"

"There is no mystery in that, Jake. Think about it. Here we are located in one of the better tourist spots in the country. A major part of my customer base is Americans and Europeans. How many of them think they will get the real Irish experience in a place called

Jacek Kozlowski's Bar rather than Jack McCarthy's Bar?"

"You've got a point there, Finbarr. Mind you, you could have a good business with Polish tourists, although there might not be too many around here."

"Ain't that right, Jake. The last polish tourist we had in Ireland was Pope John Paul and I wouldn't get rich on what he might be drinking. When you think about it, Jake, this is another example of branding. The brand name should represent what you are promising. Some brand names can entice people immediately and that is what Jack McCarthy's Bar does."

"Don't disagree with you. A good name or brand name can change attitudes, anyone's attitude. You ever hear of Toby Keith?"

Finbarr hesitated, "Not sure that I have."

"He's a country singer, back home. Sings good stuff—not that heavy metal grunge crap you listen to."

"They're different."

"Ha?"

"They're different—heavy metal and grunge are different types of music. Don't be gettin' them brand names wrong now," said a smiling Finbarr, knowing he was raising Jake's frustration level.

"Finbarr, do me a favor. Pretend you're dumb. Please. Let's get back to Toby Keith. He bumped into that grand old music man, Willie Nelson, a few months ago in a restaurant."

"Willie Nelson, I like him."

"Finbarr. DUMB ...Toby told Willie he had written a song, which he would like to record with him. A little circumspect, Willie said to Toby Keith—'Send it to me and I'll let you know. What is the song title?' Toby Keith replied, *'Beer For My Horses.'* Lyrics include *'Whiskey for my men, beer for my horses.'* Willie looked at him, didn't hesitate and said, *'Beer For My Horses,*—I'll record it with you.'"

"That, Finbarr, is an example of the power of a good brand name. Willie Nelson didn't even need to hear the song, which by the way is quite a good one, but he was enticed, enchanted, entranced even— Jeez, I'm beginning to sound Irish—by what was effectively the brand name.

"I guess a brand name that creates what might be called the 'Willie Nelson reaction' can have real impact. Makes me wonder whether I should change my brand name from *JB's Good Food* to something better."

"You know that's not the answer. Look, you've invested a lot in your brand. Even if you're not that happy with the results, there must be some equity in *JB's Good Food*. Don't throw that away unless you have a very good reason. The initials 'JB' remind me of a story about President Lyndon Baines Johnson."

"LBJ, himself."

"That's the man and you have just made my point for me."

"I have?" Jake said quizzically. "That's good to know."

"It is, isn't it? The 'LBJ' moniker did not happen by chance you know. Johnson believed that initials conveyed a certain gravitas and substance to a politician. For instance, Roosevelt was known as 'FDR.' Thus Johnson wanted to be known not as Lyndon Johnson but as 'LBJ.' Funny, isn't it, that even in the political arena, an old-timer like Johnson understood the importance of branding."

"Pity the product didn't live up to the branding."

Finbarr demurred. "I'm not too sure about that, Jake. LBJ had great qualities and achieved an awful lot, both as Senator and President—especially in terms of civil rights. His problem was his presidency was framed by the Vietnam War—something which he was not able to find a solution to. Hopefully, it won't happen in your case, but sometimes no matter how hard you try, you cannot beat your environment and the market forces that surround you—especially if you do not change strategy."

"O.K., great and wise Irish cousin, I stand corrected. Now, if only you knew how to create that magical brand image for me, I'd buy you another pint."

"Naw, this one's on me, Jake," said Finbarr, as he raised two fingers to the barman and pointed to two empty pint glasses. "Pat, two more please. My Yankee cousin has got a taste for the black stuff."

Finbarr returned to his theme.

"Jake, there are a million marketing gurus out there in guru-land. They'll be happy to take your money and tell you how to create that brand magic. The essence for some brands is simple, but making it happen is so difficult. But, when it happens … look at Harley, Starbucks, the Volkswagen Beetle. What have they got in common?"

"Great brands. Maybe they all get you 'juiced up' or moving."

"Well, aren't you the clever one now, Jake, but there's a bit more to it than that. One of the things they have in common is an element of nostalgia that is associated with the brands."

"But Starbucks is a young brand. How can that be nostalgic?"

"We'll get to Starbucks in a few minutes. Now, Jake, I'm not saying this applies to you, but most of the guys who buy Harleys are re-living their youth and their carefree days of yore. They're weekend-rebels, Jake. You're twenty-eight years old, right? Same age as I am—twenty-eight, right? You, Mr. Jake Boyd, must be one of the youngest guys to have purchased a bike from your Harley dealer. I mean the average age of a Harley purchaser is mid-forties."

"And young at heart, Finbarr. Young at heart."

"That's right. That's right. The great thing for Harley is those are the guys who have the disposable income to pay a premium of five grand. But the last thing the brand would want is to be associated with old-timers."

"I can see that. Nostalgia—yes, but not old-timers."

"The magic of Harley, Jake, is the nostalgia it evokes. The safe rebel image that the multi-million-aire Harley rider can exhibit at the weekend. That's what your five grand premium gets you. Harley sells more than three hundred thousand bikes a year, you know. More than twenty percent of those bikes are bought by buyers who have never ridden a motorbike before or not ridden one in the last five years."

"That's sixty thousand people! Every year!"

"That's right, Jake. That's right. At an average of about fifteen grand. What is it Neil Young sings, 'Somewhere on a desert highway, she rides a Harley-Davidson.' It's the dream Jake, it's the dream Harley evokes."

"It is illogical isn't it, Finbarr? Like many HOG—
that's our pet name for Harleys by the way—riders, I
don't wear a helmet. Yet you can bet that the arche-
typical no-helmet-wearing multi-millionaire lawyer
HOG rider—God that's a mouthful—you mentioned
a moment ago, will be in court during the week,
arguing the case against a motor corporation which
failed to provide adequate seat belts in a car."

"Jake, ain't that the truth. The great brands are
the ones where consumers park their brain somewhere, but drive the purchase with their heart.
Simple, isn't it?" said the smiling Irishman.

"Yeah, right. Let's stick with this nostalgia line for
a minute. The Volkswagen Beetle has some of the
same type of nostalgic feel to it, you believe?"

"That it does, man. I mean that car is nothing but
a Volkswagen Golf dressed up in a fancier livery. It is
a small car, not the best quality in the world—
although adequate, but people want it."

"I don't know if you have the PT Cruiser here in
Ireland, but the same thing happened with that car.
The demand was such that dealers could charge a
premium for it."

"And why do buyers want these cars, Jake? A lot
of it is driven by nostalgia and that never goes out of

fashion."

"Interesting, you should say that, Finbarr, because following the events of September 11, a lot of social commentators were suggesting people wanted to get back to family values, comfort food, etc."

"Yea, I read some of that, but I happen to think that was a load of psycho-mumbo-babble. Now there's a word you don't hear very often, Jake. It's an even bigger word than marmalade."

"Finbarr, if there were a profession of psycho-mumbo-babbleism, I'm sure you would punch holes in it very fast. It's a pity though that most of those iconic brands mentioned seem to be transport oriented."

"Not true, my cousin. Not true at all. Look at Starbucks. Look at Krispy Kreme and I suppose you could claim Ben & Jerry's has a certain 'it' factor as well."

"Finbarr, Starbucks amazes me. I've studied them a little because they are in the food business, but you know that is a bit like saying Harley-Davidson is just a motorcycle manufacturer. Jeez, I'm beginning to think like you now. That is worrying! Starbucks. Even though people buy coffee there, it is selling a lot more than that. It has to be, because before they came along no one would have dreamed of paying three bucks for a cup of coffee. Starbucks is selling the experience. Some people call it 'the third place'— a haven between work and home."

" 'The third place.' I like that. We call it 'the pub' here in Ireland."

"Well they both sell plenty of black liquid anyway, that's for sure. You know, Finbarr, there are almost twenty thousand possible drink options available in a Starbucks. And people think they are just selling a cup of coffee."

"Twenty thousand? Wow, maybe I should rebrand my place Starpubs. No, hold a minute, that'd be a bad idea. If something like that ever happened with Guinness, 'twould be nothing short of a national disaster. Could you imagine, my barman Pat being asked for a Grande pint of Guinness with a twist of hazelnut. Some things are better left simple, Cousin Jake. Some things are better left simple."

"Dat's right. Dat's right. Some things should not be touched," said Jake watching another pint of Guinness appear, as if by magic, in front of him. "I think I'm finding religion here, Finbarr," he said with a large smile while he reverently raised the pint of 'Black Magic' to his lips.

Jake no longer sipped his pint. He had watched with admiration as Finbarr swallowed a third of the pint in one movement and now felt comfortable enough to do the same.

"So I should be trying to create a bit of magic around *JB's Good Food* brand. I still don't know how to do it, but you've given me plenty of food for thought—and drink as well. The Krispy Kreme brand has that certain magic as well, you know, Finbarr. Those donuts really do taste good, but the brand image is much bigger and more vibrant than the actual sales would justify. They have been hit in the last few months because of this low carb craze, but prior to that problem, it seemed Krispy Kreme would conquer the world. It's another example of what you were talking about—great brands encourage consumers to park their brains. The whole world was talking about the dangers of obesity and at one stage Krispy Kreme sales were going through the roof."

"Do you know what that is called, Jake?"

"Do I know what, what is called?" said Jake with a look of total confusion.

"It's called consumption-schizophrenia—which means two things. One, is that I get the award for use of the biggest word today. The second is that consumption-schizophrenia means we, as consumers, talk about cutting back on food intake, but when we do, we reward ourselves with food for cutting back on food. Are you with me there, Cousin?"

Jake laughed. "You are full of surprises and I'm still worried that so many of the surprises make sense. But you are right, you know. Outback Steakhouse, one of the biggest restaurant chains in the U.S. provided a very good example of that recently."

"Let me guess. Outback is not a chain of Irish restaurants."

"Right once again, Finbarr."

"Give me a chance. Outback... an Australian concept? The great outback... the great outdoors. Simple concept, but very evocative though. Another example of a great brand name. Can you chase 'sheilas' there?"

"I'm sure you can, Finbarr. Their boyfriends mightn't be too impressed, but I'm sure with your ability to charm your way out of trouble, they'd break only one of your legs—at a time. What I was trying to say before you interrupted me was to give you another example of schizophrenia-consumption."

"Consumption-schizophrenia," Finbarr corrected him.

"Whatever. I think I did well even pronouncing those words with all this Guinness in me."

Finbarr nodded in agreement. "You're doing well

Jake, even if you have passed the pint of no return. Get it? 'Pint' of no return." Finbarr looked for a response from Jake, but the American's mind was not working as fast as earlier in the evening. Undaunted by the lack of appreciation of his humor, Finbarr continued. "Now tell me about this place where they chat up 'sheilas'."

Jake took a long gulp of Guinness and settled back in a self-satisfied manner. "The Outback restaurant group found that some of their older customers wanted smaller portions. So they tested smaller portions in a few restaurants and guess what?"

"What?"

"The test was so successful, Outback introduced smaller portions as a menu option on a national basis."

"Big deal. What has that got to do with consumption schizo…whatever it is?" Finbarr was also now feeling the effects of the black beverage.

"The really interesting thing, my Irish cousin, is Outback discovered that even though diners were buying the smaller portions, the check average went up. And you know why?"

"Why?"

"Previously, many of their older customers were purchasing one large entrée, sharing it between two.

Now according to the guys in Outback, diners purchase the individual smaller portion and often also purchase either an appetizer or a dessert. Now, if that ain't—let me say this slowly—con-sump-tion schizo-phren-ia, I don't know what is."

"Jake, I can't beat that."

The cousins consumed one further pint of 'Black Magic' before departing.

The police car parked surreptitiously at the end of the parking lot reinforced Finbarr's previous thinking they should walk home.

"See that cop-car over there, Jake."

The dark night and combination of alcohol elicited slow recognition from Jake.

"Waiting to catch some foolish 'pinter,' I suppose."

"That's right, but—and I promise you this will be the last brand story tonight Jake—a lot of people have this image of Ireland, where everyone goes to the pub every night of the week. I wish they would, by the way—and go home, plastered—that's drunk to you, Jake. But do you know, we have some of the most stringent drink-drive laws in the world? You get done for drunk-driving here and it's 'goodbye license' for at least one year. Smoking in pubs is outlawed, so that's another example of reality being different to the brand image. In these cases, it is a good thing, but most brands have to be careful that reality does not differ from the image. If it does differ, they're sunk."

"Finbarr," Jake said slowly.

"What?"

"When the reality differs from the image, would you call that—brand ... schizo ... schizophrenia?"

"Interesting question, that. But it'd be more like brand dislocation, I'd say."

"You know what, Finbarr, given all this schizo-phrenia and dislocation, I think we should set up a consultancy—we could call it 'Brand Doctors.' What do you think?"

"Let's do that, although we'd probably be done for malpractice. And by those no-helmet-wearing multi-millionaire lawyer buddies of yours."

"Finbarr, in the words of the late John Denver— you wouldn't know him, he could sing—'Take me home country roads'."

"Soon. Let's hit Mick's Plaice on the way home."

"What's Mick's Place?"

"Best fish and chips around, Jake. It's Mick's Plaice as in the name of the fish. P-L-A-I-C-E."

"Oh, I get it, you mean the flat fish."

A four hundred yard walk brought the cousins to Mick's Plaice. A line of people waited to enter. Every few seconds, happy boisterous groups of two's and three's left the premises, munching Mick's fish and chips with great gusto.

The line moved quickly. The alcohol slowed Jake's appreciation of his surroundings. He turned to Finbarr. "Am I dreaming? It's midnight and this place is throbbing with people. Do they have no homes to go to?"

"It's early yet for some of them. A few others are just working up the courage to go home. Relax yourself there, Jake, I'll order some good food for you."

Chapter Four

Where the Angels Swim

———— ♣ ————

Lesson:
The Brand Experience

———— ♣ ————

*"Give people a taste of Old Crow,
and tell them it's Old Crow.
Then give them another taste of
Old Crow, but tell them it's Jack Daniels.
Ask them which they prefer. They'll think
the two drinks are quite different.
They are tasting images."*

— David Ogilvy

*"Eat here, and you'll
never live to regret it."*

— Finbarr Kozlowski

Jake woke with a mild thumping in his head. The sun streaming in via the break in the bedroom curtains bathed his face. Raising his head from the pillow exaggerated the headache. He struggled out of bed, moving slowly to the shower, swearing never to drink again. Somewhere in the distance, he heard Finbarr singing gaily to himself. *Does that guy ever slow down?* he thought.

Toweling down after the shower, Jake heard Finbarr shout, "Yank, breakfast is ready—can't keep it hot all day you know." Jake said a silent prayer breakfast would be light.

Tentatively, he moved to the kitchen where Finbarr was indulging in a manic dance while holding a spatula in his hand. The pounding in Jake's head was accentuated by a wall of sound from the music system. "God, Finbarr, what is that racket?"

"It's Lars and the boys, Jake—Metallica—Great way to wake in the morning. Gets the blood going."

"Be nice to me, Finbarr. Drop the sound a bit. It's fighting with a power drill in my head. I think we had a few too many pints last night."

"Naw, you were unlucky," responded Finbarr as he lowered the volume slightly. "You probably got one bad pint in among the other six. Here, eat this breakfast. It'll set you up for the day."

"Oh God, what is this?"

"You said you wanted an Irish breakfast. Three slices of black pudding—blood pudding to you—a few slices of bacon, mushrooms, baked beans, two giant sausages from McBrides the Butcher and two fresh eggs, sunny side up as you guys like to say, ready to drip all over your toast. Get that down ya and you'll be ready to go rockin' 'n' rollin' all day."

Jake made a feeble effort at breakfast. Finbarr—regularly interrupted by calls on his cell phone—did not sit for long. Jake slowly, very slowly, felt better.

"Finbarr, I need to check my email. Mind if I go on line?"

"Away you go. It's a wireless set up, so go into the front room if you wish."

Jake returned fifteen minutes later. "Can't get

access for some reason. I'll try later. What's the plan for today? I might do my 'Nixon thing' and do some thinking based on all the advice you gave me yesterday. And you, any plans?"

"I'm trying to keep the week clear because you are visiting. I've got to go down to the petrol station for a few hours around mid-day, because we have a short term staff issue. Just for a few hours though. We do well here in terms of staff—in both the pub and petrol station, but it's pretty tough to keep things going. Unemployment in this country is only about four percent and in busy areas, like tourist areas during the summer, there is such a shortage of good people, I tell you—Stevie Wonder could get a job as a traffic cop."

Finbarr continued with his activities. Jake opted for a brief walk, partly to help clear his head but also to escape from the overpowering enthusiasm of Finbarr. Small white clouds gave Jake some cover from a sun that drenched the countryside in bright light. To Jake's astonishment, the driver of every car that passed waved a warm greeting. Refreshed, he returned to the house.

"Feeling better, Jake? I told you them runny eggs would get the blood circulating. Remember, we have to walk down to the petrol station, so get your hiking boots on, or whatever you walk in."

The walk to the village seemed much longer than last night's journey home. Maybe, Jake thought, it is because he did not remember much of the previous night's final hours.

Entering the petrol station, Finbarr shouted to the attractive young lady at the cash register. "Howz it goin', Fiona? No problems?"

"Not a bother, Finbarr. It's going fine. We've been busy this morning. Nearly one-hundred-fifty cars so far." Looking at Jake, she said, "So this is your American cousin, is it? Hi, I'm Fiona. Finbarr hasn't led you too far astray, I hope."

"Hi Fiona, good to meet you. We've got a saying back home, 'What happens in Vegas, stays in Vegas', so I think I'll take the Fifth on that."

"Oh, it was one of those nights, was it? Finbarr, I'm sorry about you coming in today, but I've got my I.T. exam at two o'clock."

"Don't worry about that, Fiona. You gave me plenty notice and your brother will be here in a few hours anyway. Off you go and get top marks now, kiddo."

"I'll do that, Finbarr. Jake, hope to see you again, soon."

Jake watched Fiona as she mounted her bicycle

gracefully and swiftly pedaled off. "She's a cutie, Finbarr, I think I'm in love. I can see what General Paddy meant about the Irish colleens seducing the invaders."

"Jake, you can get seduced all you like, but she's going with Gerry O'Regan, who as well as being the local cop, is about six-foot-two. I'm sure you could handle him though, even if he has a black belt in judo."

"Maybe I should play to my strengths, Finbarr and not tackle that issue. I've enough problems of my own. She's doing some computer course?"

"She is. She's doing a Masters degree—computer science or something like that. She's a bright kid, but so is her brother. You'll meet him soon. He's studying some kind of computer program also. He already has job offers from Microsoft, Intel and Dell, when he finishes next year. All of them companies have major facilities in Ireland."

"Yeah, I keep reading about the Celtic Tiger. Seems as if this country never stops growing economically."

"The last twenty years have been great for the economy, all right. We have one of the best educated workforces in the western world, which is why so many high tech companies have invested here. That can cause its own problems though."

"What do you mean?" said Jake, as he sipped coffee that was surprisingly good for a gas station.

"Somewhere, in the recesses of my mind, I think we were speaking about 'brand dislocation' last night. Do you remember?"

"Was that only last night? I think I remember the phrase."

"Well, the funny thing about Ireland is that the guys who are trying to sell this country now have two major conflicting images they wish to get across. You have one group of people in the Irish development agencies who wish to convey Ireland as one of the most advanced economies in the world in terms of education, telecommunications infrastructure, ease of access—all that kind of stuff, like. Then you have the guys in the Irish Tourist Board who persuade the world that Ireland is a lovely, sleepy, easy going location where you can forget the trials and pace of everyday living."

"Hey, that's not a difficult sell. Seems both parties are succeeding. How can that be?"

"Well, realistically, Jake, they are selling two different products, even if it's the same brand name. The two products are supported by different marketing and ad campaigns, each with real consistency.

And I suppose, the target markets are different. In any event, it seems to have worked so far and long may it continue."

Finbarr glanced out at the forecourt.

"Sometimes, Cousin, the image needs some rein-forcement. Watch this."

Finbarr moved swiftly, raising the volume level on the monitor which was panning the gas pumps. Reaching under the counter, he grabbed a thick white Aran sweater, which he quickly slipped over his head. Before Jake could say anything, Finbarr was out the door walking briskly to the silver BMW pulled up beside pump two. Finbarr looked incongruous wear-ing the thick woolen sweater that was about three sizes too large for him. Jake noticed that Finbarr was now wearing a brown woolen cap pulled over his ears. This was not the ideal clothing for a warm day. He watched the monitor and listened with rising incredulity. Finbarr was speaking in a stronger brogue than normal. "Howz it go-ann there, lads? Is it some petrol you want?"

Two large men exited from the car and stretched. Jake recognized the East Coast accents.

"Yea Mac, we shure do. And we're looking to get to the gwalf course. We can't use Mapquest around here."

"And what would we be needin' that for, Sir?

Doesn't everyone around here know where every-place is, around here like? But I'll tell ya how to get to the golf course.

"If you go down this road for about two miles, you'll see a road to the right. That road takes you over the beautiful green hillside an' you'll get a great view of the lakes. They say it is where the angels swim."

Finbarr paused.

"Don't take that road. Half a mile before that road, there is a turn to the left—take that, and the golf course is about three kilometers down there."

The driver listened intently to Finbarr. "You Irish. You give directions in kilometers and the odometer in the car is in miles."

"Confusing, isn't it?" said Finbarr. "Have you gentlemen visited these parts before?"

"No Mac, we haven't, although I shure do love it. My grandfather emigrated from here years ago. I remember sitting on his knee and he telling me about the beautiful Irish people and countryside. He never told me about the great Irish gwalf courses you guys have."

"They're good alright, so I'm told," Finbarr said, "and you know there are some great pubs around here as well. You should visit Jack McCarthy's Bar after the golf game. It's just down the road there. Great food and great Guinness."

"Hey, we might just do that. You don't own it or anything do you?"

"Ah now sir, that'd be tellin'."

The American driver shook Finbarr's hand profusely.

"Thanks a lot for your help, Mac. Shure do appreciate it."

"You're more than welcome, Sir. God speed. Keep an eye out for sheep on the road, when you are near the golf course."

"Sheep on the road, I've heard it all now," he gestured to his associate as both Americans got into the car.

Finbarr moved swiftly back to the gas station. Jake looked at him in wonder.

"What was that all about?"

"Let me take this sweater off first. I'm meltin'. Got to make a quick phone call." He hit a speed dial button on his cell phone.

"Hi Mick? Finbarr. How you doing?... I'm doing great, man. Quick one for you. I've just had a couple of Yanks at the station. Really nice guys. Are you out on the land at the moment?... Good. Good. Look, they'll be going by your place in about ten minutes.

Put a few sheep out on the road for them. Give them a touch of old Ireland ... don't worry, you'll hear them coming. They're driving a rental stick shift ... O.K., see you sometime. Keep the shovel tippin'. Cheers."

Finbarr tossed the cell phone on the bench in front of him.

"Now, are you going to tell me what that was all about?" repeated Jake.

"It's the brand experience, Jake. Those guys came looking for the *real* Ireland. Aran sweaters. Friendly people. Crazy directions. That's the brand he wanted to see. I'm helping him experience the brand promise."

"And what's with the sheep?"

"Sheep? That's added value. The driver was good enough to offer me a cigar—didn't take it—but I just thought it'd be a nice memory for him to have—to give sheep the right-of-way on our highways and by-ways. Remember that brand magic we were talking about yesterday, Harley-Davidson and Starbucks, Jake. Ireland has got an 'it' factor as well you know. Sometimes, there is no harm in reinforcing it. Maybe, all of this will help get you thinking, about how you can create an 'it' factor around your brand. Create the 'it' factor and it will pay dividends eventually."

"Finbarr, I think you must be the sanest nutcase

I've met in my life."

Time passed swiftly as a steady procession of cars stopped for gas and supplies. Finbarr dealt with all customers in an easy, friendly manner. At five minutes to two, a long haired youth opened the station door. His T-shirt read 'Michael Flatley kicks for Ireland.'

"Hi Finbarr, you haven't been working too hard now, I hope."

"Jimmy, I'm exhausted—two hours of surveying my empire is too much for me at my age. You're O.K. for the afternoon, yea?"

"No problem at all Finbarr, why shouldn't I be?" He looked at Jake, extended his hand, "Hi, I'm Jimmy Shea. Finbarr says I'm his 'Apprentice', ever since he saw that Donald Trump program. Only difference is that Finbarr has more dosh than Trump. Doesn't have all the babes though. Doesn't have the hair either."

"Hi, I'm Jake. Jake Boyd—I'm a relation of this Irish version of Donald Trump."

"Oh yea, that's right, I heard you were in town. I believe you gave it a bit of a belter in the pub last night."

"News travels fast around these parts. Good job I didn't misbehave too much."

"Well, from what I hear, you lads were in no condition to be doing anything."

Turning to Finbarr, Jimmy explained, "Gerry O'Regan just called up to the house. Bring Fiona to her exams you know. Told me you guys were in rare ol' form last night."

"Yeah, I saw the car in the car park when we were leaving. Tell me, is O'Regan going to make an honest man of your sister? If he doesn't, Jake here is going to move in."

"Who knows, Finbarr? Although I'd be careful if I were you, Jake, Gerry's got a black belt in judo. He's about six foot three and built like Pat Murphy's bull."

"Oh—ho," said Finbarr. "Fiona would want to be careful. He could do her a lot of damage so."

"Will ya give over! That's my sister you're talkin' about. No, fair's, fair. Gerry is a nice guy like, but you wouldn't want to get on the wrong side of him, you know."

"I'm getting the picture," said a resigned Jake. Finbarr collected his cell phone. "Right. Jimmy, we're off. Don't burn the place down now."

Chapter Five

Genchi Genbutsu

---　♣　---

Lesson:
Go to the Source
and Learn

---　♣　---

He (Michael Jackson) would watch tapes of gazelles and cheetahs and panthers to imitate the natural grace of their movement.

—Quincy Jones

A s they walked from the gas station, Jake turned to Finbarr.

"Does everyone know everyone's business here, Finbarr?"

"Naw. No one is interested unless it has to do with sex, drugs, rock 'n' roll, religion, sport, education, money or your neighbor. Apart from that no one bothers anyone else—unless of course, it's interesting. Mind you, Jake, you might learn something from it though."

"How?"

"Well, like, in a sense, it's a kind of market research—people know what is going on in their space. Businesses need to have the same kind of philosophy. Understanding customers, understanding your space is critical to staying alive."

Jake nodded in agreement. "Trouble is, it costs to know what is happening. I don't have sufficient budget to really understand my customers."

"Aw, poor old Jake. You haven't got sufficient budget? That is a load of old hogwash. We were talking about President Lyndon Johnson the other day. I'll tell you another story about LBJ. When he went to Washington first as a congressional aide, he stayed in the Dodge Hotel with a number of seasoned congressional aides. Johnson's biographer, a guy called Robert Dallek, says Johnson showered four times the first evening."

"He must have been pretty clean by the time he was finished."

"He might have been, but that's not why he did it. This was the 1930s and the hotel had only communal facilities. Each time Johnson showered, he queried different aides as to what was happening in Washington, who the movers and shakers were and who got things done. LBJ had his finger on the pulse all his life and spent a lot of time understanding his market. But think about it. That shower incident only cost time—no expense involved—but the result was that Johnson substantially improved his knowledge of his market. Jake, you *can* find out what is happening in your market. Spend time in the supermarket aisles. Talk to people who shop your section. Keep asking questions."

Finbarr hesitated, searching for words. "Who's that baseball guy that makes all the stupid statements?"

"George Steinbrenner?"

"No, no—the guy with the name like the cartoon bear—Yogi Berra, that's him. He once said, 'You can observe a lot by watching.' You know, Jake, he is absolutely right. The good companies observe and learn. Look at the Toyota Motor Corporation. It has a concept called *Genchi Genbutsu,* which means, 'Go to the source and learn.' You can call it management by walking around if you want to—but—Jake, *don't* tell me that you haven't got enough money to do research. The bigger the research budget, the more out of touch some companies become.

"Look at all the brouhaha about low carb. You said yourself it may be affecting your business. I don't think any of the large food companies saw it coming despite their much vaunted—what do they call 'em—'consumer insight' groups.

"Look at Unilever. Sales of one of their most profitable brands—Slim-Fast—fell by over twenty percent because customers moved to low carb products. That was a one billion dollar brand and they missed the low carb craze. Can you imagine how much they spend on research?"

Jake did not have an opportunity to answer. Finbarr was on one of his animated rants. Without pausing for breath, he continued.

"Look at McDonald's prior to their current turn-around. It proudly proclaimed it conducted over two-hundred-thousand mystery shopper visits in their U.S. stores every year—yet the business was going down the toilet faster than you could say, 'Big Mac and fries, please.'

"Jake, *the* critical thing is to be inquisitive. Michael Dell did not start with a large research budget. Steve Jobs in Apple did not have a large budget, but he understood what Apple customers wanted, because he—like Michael Dell—kept asking what I call 'dumb questions.'"

Finbarr stopped walking and looked intently at the American. "Except Jake," he said, poking him in the chest, "there is no such thing as dumb questions when it comes to your market. There is just dumb analysis of the answers. Maybe there is also a Mr. Magoo factor. Manufacturers fail to see, or fail to believe what they see. Not one of the U.S. car manufacturers—when they did dominate the world market, saw the need for smaller, more fuel efficient cars. How can three giants miss that type of paradigm shift?"

"Paradigm shift. We *are* getting wordy, aren't we?"

"Ha! I suppose so. I've often wondered what phrase was used before 'paradigm shift.' But companies miss these shifts so often. IBM didn't understand laptops, the major airlines didn't understand the low fare market, and look at the fast food industry. Most of the fast food industry was slow to respond to changing consumer needs, until Wendy's introduced their *Garden Sensation Salads*."

"And now everyone is introducing salads."

"That's right. That's right. Jake, many companies spend more on market research in a minute than you could in a year and yet are slow to react. You—as a small manufacturer can have a tactile appreciation of the market, which the big guys may not have."

"I can have a what?"

"A tactile appreciation of the market. Kind of, means you should be able to touch, feel, smell, breathe, your customer's wants and needs."

"And I do that by asking dumb questions?"

"Yup, but try and ask a few intelligent ones also, but you know what I mean. Just make sure you ask the right questions and of the right people also. Do you remember 'Mighty Mick,' the Ryanair CEO. He's getting rid of reclining seats on Ryanair aircraft because of the maintenance cost involved. Ryanair conducted a survey on reclining seats. What question, Jake, did they ask customers about reclining seats?

'Do you like reclining seats? Would you be happy if your seat was not able to recline?'

"This is what I mean by asking the right questions, Jake. If you ask airline customers would they be happy if reclining seats were removed, the majority would answer, 'No, I want a reclining seat.' However if you pose the question as Ryanair did, 'Would you be satisfied if the person in front could not recline their seat in your face?' Guess what? Ninety-four percent said, 'Yes.' Now I reckon Ryanair would probably get rid of those reclining seats in any event, because of the cost implications and their manic drive to be the low cost airline, but my point is that you must take care crafting your questions and ask those questions of the right people."

"Do you mind if we make this a dialogue, Finbarr?"

"You're not suggesting I'm goin' on a bit, are you? No one's ever said that before!"

"I doubt that. You've never heard anyone say it, as you rambled on. You know, people can read things the wrong way. Not you, Finbarr, of course, but other people. One of our greatest presidents—FDR—when seeking election for the third time rebuked a friend for never voting Democrat. The friend's response was, 'Mr. President, the first time you won, I voted Republican—the economy improved. The second time you won, I also voted Republican and the economy continued to improve. I've never had it so good. Why change a winning formula?' "

Finbarr nodded, appreciating the anecdote.

"You've been hanging around with your multi-millionaire lawyer buddies too much. That's their type of logic."

"Learning from you, Finbarr. Tell me, did you ever read *Ulysses* by James Joyce?"

"Never did. Why?"

"That's the trouble with you Irish. You read everything but Irish writers. There is a scene in *Ulysses* which is relevant to your rant about the correct response. One of the female characters goes to confession and tells the priest her boyfriend touched her. The priest asked, 'Where did he touch you, my child?'

'On the bank of the river, Father.' "

"Oh, I like it, Jake. The dangers of open-ended questions. Could you imagine the priest going back to his bishop saying, 'Hey "Bish," I think we have a problem with these open-ended questions.' There is another oldie but goldie about the confessional which highlights information gathering."

"What's that?"

"Well, this guy—let's call him Mick, not 'Mighty Mick' now—goes to confession and tells the priest he has misbehaved with a young lady. The priest gets inquisitive and asks for the girl's name. Mick, being an honorable guy, says he couldn't divulge that type of information."

"He took the Fifth—in confession. That's a pretty novel approach."

"I suppose it is, but anyway, the priest was a little annoyed at this and probed further. 'Tell me, my son, was it Mary O'Rourke?'

'Ah, no, Father.'

'Was it Elizabeth O'Brien?'

'No, Father, no.'

'Mary Haughey?'

'No, Father—I'd rather not say.'

Finally Mick left the confessional where he met his buddy, Brendan. 'How'd it go in there, Mick?'

'Not too bad, not too bad at all. He went easy on me and I've got three good leads for tonight.'"

"Finbarr, that is so lame, but I see your point.

Basically what you are saying is that you can find information in many different ways."

"That's right. That's right. Sure it's a silly example, but in real life, most businesses see the same information. The company that deciphers information best and knows how to use information has a better chance of success."

"Good point. Makes me wonder what time confession happens in this town?"

Chapter Six

The Dreamers of the Day

---- ♣ ----

Lesson:
Never Give Up

---- ♣ ----

" I haven't failed.
I've found 10,000 ways
that don't work. "

—Thomas Edison

J ake logged out of his email and rose slowly from the table. He did not move with the renewed fluency and energy which had characterized his movement in recent days.

A concerned Finbarr watched him slump into a soft chair. "You look like a guy who's just lost the winning lotto ticket, Jake. What's up?"

"It's not far off that, Finbarr. Just checked my email. Our largest account says if we don't develop a strategy that promises growth in the next quarter, it's 'Goodnight'. How are we supposed to turn this around? It's time ... to talk to Vultures from Hell," Jake said despondently.

Finbarr shifted forward in his chair, and grabbed his cousin's arm firmly. "Jake, one thing is certain. You will *not* succeed if you do not want to succeed.

And you will not succeed if you do not clarify what you want to do ...You're a movie buff, aren't you?"

"Yeah, but I am in no mood to see a movie."

"Not askin' you. Ever seen 'Lawrence of Arabia'?"

"A long time ago, Finbarr. My dad took me. Kept telling me Peter O'Toole was Irish. He was really chuffed at that. An English hero played by an Irishman."

"That's right. That's right. The movie was loosely based on T.E. Lawrence's book, *Seven Pillars of Wisdom*. In that book, Lawrence wrote:

'All men dream, but not equally. Those who dream by night in the dusty recesses of their mind wake in the day to find that it was vanity, but the dreamers of the day are dangerous men for they may act their dream with open eyes, and make it possible.'"

Finbarr looked earnestly at his relative.

"Jake, do *not* give up on your dream."

He paused.

"My very good friend, you ... you *must* become a dangerous man again, you must dream with open eyes and make it possible.

"Tell you what. Let's just take it easy this evening. We'll talk about it tomorrow. You want to watch a good Metallica DVD?"

"Only if they smash their guitars."

"Who."

"What?"

"The Who. It was The Who who smashed their guitars, not Metallica. I gotta educate you, man."

"Whatever... I think I'll go for a walk—on my own if you don't mind." Finbarr consented. Pangs of emotion moved through his body as he watched his cousin walk slowly, shoulders slightly hunched, toward the door.

"Hey, Jake, you're not sneaking off for a little tete-a-tete with Fiona now, are you?"

A sliver of a smile decorated Jake's face. "I wish!" Jake slowly walked the moonlit road. A calm aura enveloped the countryside, reinforced by the rustle of small animals moving swiftly, expertly, through the dense undergrowth that bordered the roadside. Moonlight bathed the adjacent fields in a mellow glow. *Maybe this is the answer,* thought Jake. *Sell the business and emigrate to Ireland. General Paddy was right. This country does seduce people.*

He returned to the house, feeling no better, unsure what decision he might take. Refusing the 'wimp coffee' Finbarr offered, Jake wished him 'goodnight' and climbed the stairs.

He did not notice the envelope on his pillow until

sitting to ease himself into bed. The white envelope had one word written in a large scrawl—'Yank.' Holding it in his hand for a few moments, he debated whether he wanted any more of Finbarr's incessant enthusiasm. Finally, curiosity got the better of him. He pulled a card from the envelope. A hand-written smiling face was the only graphic on the face of the card. Jake opened the card:

Never give up, never give up
Never, Never, Never, Never
Give in, to things great or small, large or petty
Except to conviction of honour and good sense
  —Winston Churchill, Harrow school,
    November 1942

'Jake—Your buddy Churchill had the right idea. Hang in there. I love you, man. —Finbarr.'

Jake pulled the bed clothes to his shoulder. Five minutes after he switched the light, he was in a deep sleep.

Chapter Seven

The Mobile Disco

--- ♣ ---

Lesson:
Attitude

--- ♣ ---

We are all in the gutter, but some of us are looking at the stars.

—Oscar Wilde,
Lady Windermere's Fan

"Well, the top of the mornin' to you, Jake. I'm not even down the stairs and I see your ugly mug already. Did ya not sleep?"

"Far from it, Finbarr. I went out like a light. Didn't wake until I heard that dumb cock crow."

"Never need an alarm clock around here, do ya? Tell you what. Quick cup of coffee and we're outta here."

"Suits me. What's the plan?"

"No idea. Into the car and wherever it takes us. I know it isn't the clarity of vision I've been giving you hell about, but who's checkin'?"

The car moved swiftly through the Irish countryside. Jake begged Finbarr to reduce the volume on the CD player. "You've no culture, Jake. That's Motorhead. They've been damaging eardrums for years—one of the original metal bands. The lead singer is a head-banger—Lemmy Kilmister. But I'll respect your wishes. Do you want me to play some requiem music?"

Finbarr reached to change the music. "Aah, bollix," he exclaimed.

"What's wrong?"

"There's a mobile disco on my tail."

"A what?"

"Cop-car. Flashing lights. Bollix anyway. Right, let's pull in and see what's the story?"

Jake maneuvered in his seat in order to see the police car in the side mirror. A thin police officer, about the same age as the two cousins, exited the car and walked slowly to Finbarr. He bent slightly and scanned the car. "Howz it go-ann lads? You've been doing a fair clip there. I suppose you're going to a funeral or something?"

"Ah ... no, Guard, no. Can't say we are. I've got my Yankee cousin here in the car. I guess we just got too carried away with conversation. What was I doing?"

"Forty in a thirty-zone."

"Oh, oh, oh. That isn't too bright, now is it?"

"No, sir, it is not. If you keep driving like that, there may well be a funeral. And no one wants that now, do they? License and insurance, please."

The police officer looked at the documents. "Sir, your insurance is expired."

Jake shifted uneasily and with surprise when he heard Finbarr's response. "My wife looks after that, she mustn't have put the insurance certificate in the glove box."

Finbarr hesitated for a moment, then asked, "Did I meet you somewhere previously? Are you a mate of Gerry O'Regan?"

The police officer relaxed visibly. "You know him? The black belt guard? We graduated together."

"Gerry! He's a good buddy of mine. You want to take it easy on me. I'll tell him I met you, so to speak."

The policeman smiled at Finbarr. "Good try, but it doesn't work that way. Tell you what, you don't look like a guy who drives without insurance. We'll give you the benefit on that one. Speeding is going to cost you though. Here's your ticket and take it easy, will ya? I don't care if you end up going to your funeral, but it is normally other people who get hurt. If this is the worst thing that happens to you today, it won't be a bad day."

Finbarr glanced at the ticket. "Yikes, one hundred euro! Do you know how many pints of Guinness I could get for a hundred euro? Not that I'd be driving or anything after it."

"You'd get about twenty five pints in the local pub around here, but those publicans can do without your money this week. Those guys have enough money as it is."

"When I see Gerry, who'll I say done me?"

"Dave Murphy. We used kick lumps out of each other when playing football, but I like the guy a lot, even if he is a giant ugly galoot. I hear he's going out with a beaut."

"He is that. Fiona Shea—she works for me some-times. How can I face her, when she hears I got done for speedin' by a buddy of her boyfriend?"

"Hopefully, she'll tell you to slow down. I like your attitude Mr. Kozlowski. I appreciate you not giving any hassle. You wouldn't believe the crap I put up with when I stop speeding drivers. Drive safely lads. Enjoy your stay in Ireland, sir."

"I already am, Officer, I already am."

Finbarr put the car in gear and drove off at a deliberate pace.

"I suppose he's right. There are worse things that could happen. What you say, Jake?"

"I'm surprised you don't get stopped more often, to be honest, Finbarr. That cop was O.K., though."

"I guess so. Shows what happens when I believe

my own blarney. Doesn't it?"

"The Lord works in mysterious ways, and just to prove it … you know how to make a patrol cop approachable?"

"Not sure what we're talkin' about now, Jake."

"Goes back to our brand discussion and Harley in particular. I've got a couple of buddies who are patrol-cops, like that guy back there, except they spend their time on motor-bikes—Harley's Electra Glide model. Those guys say the Harley is the greatest icebreaker ever. Women even approach them and ask for a ride on the motor-bike. From a cop they don't know! It's not unusual when they cite drivers for traffic offenses, that the offenders spend more time asking about the Harley than querying the reason they've been stopped."

"It really is some brand, isn't it? A means of transport, an icebreaker, a chick magnet, an American icon—all in one great image."

"Speaking of image, Finbarr, where did your wife come from?"

Finbarr chuckled quietly. "I was debating whether I'd use that line, but it's about knowing your market, Jake. I am insured, but cops know that a lot of men leave the insurance details to their wives. I was looking for a bit of sympathy there. Got it, I guess.

Suppose I can't complain about the speeding fine. That might be overdue. Believing my own blarney, as you say. Let's turn up the sound level, Couz, and enjoy the rest of the day."

"I'm curious. Did you really meet that cop before?"

Finbarr grinned again. "Never set eyes on the guy in my life. But he looks roughly the same age as O'Regan and his ID number is pretty close to Gerry's as well, so I said I would hop the ball and see what might happen, like. It nearly worked. Goes back to what I've been saying, Jake. There is no such thing as a dumb question. Be alert to what is happening around you—your marketplace, in effect, and you will benefit. Now—let's rock 'n' roll."

Jake breathed deeply. "Finbarr, is there anything that upsets you? How do you keep your buoyant attitude?"

"It's the drugs, and the sex of course."

Jake looked quizzically.

"I'm jokin'. Lighten up a bit. Attitude is a frame of mind. Some lucky people are born with a good attitude—but even if not, you can still choose your attitude."

"What do you mean?"

"You heard of Viktor Frankl? No? He was an

Austrian psychiatrist who spent a number of years in Nazi concentration camps during the Second World War."

"Just because he was a Jew?"

"Sick world, isn't it? He was lucky enough to survive. After the war he published a book *Man's Search for Meaning*. In that book, he wrote:

'Everything can be taken from a man except the last of his freedoms, the ability to choose one's attitude in any circumstances.' "

" 'The ability to choose one's attitude in any circumstances.' Nice words, Finbarr, but simplistic, surely."

"If you don't take it in the proper context, it might sound that way, but listen to the preceding sentence that Frankl wrote:

'We who lived in the concentration camps can remember the people who walked through the huts comforting others and giving their last piece of bread. They were few in number, but they provided sufficient proof that everything can be taken from a man except the last of his freedoms—the ability to choose one's attitude in any circumstances.'

"Now, Jake, if Viktor Frankl believed people could choose their attitude in the hell-hole of a concentration camp, I reckon *we* can also choose our attitude."

"That's pretty powerful logic, Finbarr. How do you suggest we do it? Just wake in the morning, turn a switch and say, 'I'm going to get me some PMA,' you know, positive mental attitude."

"If only it was that easy. Although I am considering launching a product called *Irish Attitude*. Can you imagine it? A leprechaun and a shamrock on the label, and a brand promise that says, 'One bottle of this product and you'll feel Irish forever. Guaranteed PMA.'"

"I thought you already sold that. Is that not Guinness?"

"Ha! You might have a point there. With *Irish Attitude*, we'd keep the cost down. Water only, but premium price, like. Then again, another option could be to sell bottled Irish air. What do you think of that? Sniff genuine Irish air and inherit the attitude and the magic of The Emerald Isle. Premium price again. Offer it in pint and half-pint. Six-packs. Sell well, I reckon."

"Naturally, Finbarr. When you're finished with all this blarney, do you have any good advice on choosing your attitude?"

"Sure."

"You going to tell me?"

"Of course."

"I'm returning to the States in a few days. You'll let me know by then, I hope."

"I'll do better than that. I'll tell you now, Jake. One thing bugs me about all the gurus who tell us to have a positive mental attitude. They rarely say *how* to achieve it. Like you said—you're expected to just, you know—switch it on. The only problem with that concept is we are human beings, which means we're emotional beings. You're emotional. I'm emotional. That cop back there is emotional. That means that you and I, and everyone else, often need a catalyst to get to a positive attitude."

"Hey, I've really got you going, Finbarr."

"That's right. That's right. Many of these attitude gurus are about as helpful as someone who shows you the Grand Canyon and says, 'You should build a bridge across it.' The person then walks away and expects you to figure out how to make it happen."

"O.K., Dr. Sigmund Freud, what is your solution?"

"What do you want your attitude to be, Jake?"

"You're just asking dumb questions now, Finbarr. What do you think I want my attitude to be? I want to be pissed off and annoyed at the world all the time, so I can be miserable and fed up."

"Aw, poor little Jake is getting upset. Remember,

yesterday, I said there is no such thing as a dumb question. Now, what do really want your attitude to be?"

"O.K. O.K. I would like to be positive and believe that things are going to go right for me. You happy now?"

"Yup—and remember that dumb question you said I asked. That—my Yankee friend, Cousin, Guinness-drinking buddy of mine, is the question you need to ask yourself every single day. 'What do I want my attitude to be?' Look at your response. You initially gave a sarcastic answer that you wanted to be pissed off and annoyed with life. Not too many people will respond in that manner, unless like you, they're being sarcastic.

"The normal response will be 'I want to feel good. I want to feel positive.' Jake when you answer the question, 'What do I want my attitude to be?' in that way, you are on the first rung of the ladder to a positive mental attitude. Even if you answer in a slightly different way and you say, 'I do not want to be sad, I do not want to be annoyed, I do not want to be upset,' in some ways that is an even better response, because you quite probably will make some effort *not* to be sad, *not* to be annoyed and *not* to be upset.

"Let's go back to that speed cop. Have you ever been done for speeding over there in the land of the greenback?"

"Who hasn't? You need to be a saint, or dead, not to fall foul of traffic cops at some stage," laughed Jake.

"What was your reaction, your attitude, when you got pulled?"

"I tell you, I was not nearly as laid back as you were. Last time I got pulled for speeding, it was immediately, *immediately* after some guy passed me driving about twenty miles an hour faster than I was going—and he wasn't cited! *Grrr!* I was not impressed, especially when the cop did not accept my viewpoint. He got pretty aggressive with me. I reckon he wrote that ticket up for as much as he could."

"What good did all the frustration, all the anger do you? Nothing. Zap. Zero. Nada. That's where it got you, Jake. If—before the cop spoke to you, you had asked yourself the question, 'What do I want my attitude to be?' what would you have answered?"

"Well, I wouldn't have answered, 'I want to be happy about this?' "

"That is probably true, so what would you have answered?"

"Realistically... I guess I would have said, or I

should have said, 'I don't want to be annoyed and pissed off—because I doubt if it will help me.'"

"That's right. That's right. If you had answered the question in that way, what do you think the outcome might have been?"

"I don't know, but the cop probably would not have given me such a hard time. He might not have written the ticket the way he did, either."

"*Now* you are getting it, Jake. *The* most important question to ask yourself every day is, 'What do I want my attitude to be?' That question will help when you are stuck in traffic jams, that question will help when you are stuck in security lines at airports and that question will definitely help as you think about your business and plans for the future.

"Look, you are unsure—and I do understand why —about the future of your company, but let's do a little exercise here. What do you want your attitude to be, about your 'love child,' as you call it—your company?"

"What do you think? I want to hold onto it, I want to make it happen. I want to launch new products, expand the business. I want retailers to say, 'Give me more product now,' rather than questioning our strategy. I want to reward my employees properly. I want my customers to say that *JB's Good Food* is *it.*

That's what I want. I want to build a business that I can pass on to my kids and family."

"Now. Now, Jake. Keep Fiona out of this conversation. Seriously though, listen to what you are saying. Listen to the passion in your voice. Listen to your vision. That is all coming from the question, 'What do I want my attitude to be?' Jake, that question can change your view of life. Quite possibly even change your life."

Chapter Eight

Lemmy and Motorhead

--- ♣ ---

Lesson:
Innovation

--- ♣ ---

"Pretty much, Apple and Dell are the only ones in this industry making money. They make it by being Wal-Mart. We make it by innovation."

—Steve Jobs

“**H**ere, have a look at that article.”

Jake flinched as the magazine Finbarr threw seemed destined for his left eye.

“Hey, take it easy, Finbarr. You trying to do me some permanent damage?”

“Thought that had been done already, Jake. I mean, you like country music.”

“Very funny. What am I looking at?”

“Page thirty-three. There is a piece on innovation and the failure rates associated with new products. Thought you might be interested in it as you plan your new product strategy. The new strategy that will build *JB's Good Food* to a world class brand. Isn't that right, Jake?”

“If you say so, Einstein. Need a bit more help from you though. Play dumb now and let me read this."

Jake flicked through the magazine searching for the article. He spent quiet moments reading. Finished, he lay the magazine at his feet.

"Tell me something I don't know, Finbarr. Over ninety percent of new products fail. I'm not sure how these stats are compiled, but there seems general agreement that most new products never get far out of the starting blocks. *JB's Good Food* has a better track record than the ninety percent failure rate. But, Finbarr, it is tough. And we spend so much time and effort."

"And money," Finbarr chipped in.

"And money, that's right, on development, often for little return. We don't use outside help in developing products, but it amazes me that so many new product consulting firms generate good revenues when results in general are so poor."

"I guess you're right, Jake. When I come back in the next life, I want to either be a bull or a consultant. Many of them just end up screwing their clients and then walk away with a big happy grin on their face."

"Lovely analogy, Finbarr, but you are being a little unfair there—at least to the bull."

"Aye. Maybe so. Why did you introduce all those new products—the ones that failed? Did you really

♣

believe they were going to succeed?"

"Gee, thanks for the sensitive questioning. We had a pretty good feeling about most of them, and we also believed we needed to freshen the range."

"It's Lemmy and Motorhead all over again, Jake?"

"Ah, hello there, Finbarr. I thought we were speaking about new products and innovation, not that long haired weirdo from way back when. I knew those noise levels would damage you—although I thought it would be the ears, not the brain that would go."

Finbarr shook his head in mock despair. "Oh, ye of little faith, Jake. Too many consumer goods companies adopt what I call the Lemmy and Motorhead approach to new product launches. Is it not fair to suggest that the vast majority of new products on supermarket shelves—and indeed everywhere else—are basically line extensions?"

"Can't say for certain, but I reckon there is some truth in it."

"Darn right, there's truth in it. It is basically line extension management by month and year. In other words—Lemmy."

Jake's face displayed a puzzled frown. Finbarr repeated himself, this time laying emphasis on the first letter of key words. "Line Extension

Management by Month and Year. L – E – M – M –Y.

"I'll tell you why Lemmy and Motorhead are a good analogy for all of this. I saw the band in concert a few years back. Great gig it was, a lot of anticipation beforehand, then Motorhead came on stage, created a whole lot of noise, and a lot of excitement for the time they were there. Then they left and that was it. On to their next gig—Woodstock, or whatever the equivalent for aging rockers is these days.

"Jake, most new product launches are just like that. There is a lot of noise and excitement around the new product, prior to and during the launch period. But invariably, almost as soon as the launch period is over—once the band leaves the stage, as it were, attention moves away because thoughts and effort move to the next gig. In the business world, the new product is often left to fend for itself and a new level of excitement and noise is created around the next big thing.

"A lot of products are launched to fill a void in company plans, *not* to fill a void in the market place. Isn't it amazing the number of companies, the number of brands, that have innovation plans which call for new products to be launched every quarter or some other defined period? What that results in, is a mad dash to fill an innovation pipeline, so that the responsible managers are seen to be doing their job.

"A high percentage of new products are launched, Jake, not to satisfy a market demand but to satisfy management demand. That is one of the reasons why many new products fail."

"I don't doubt your wisdom, 'Great and Wise Guru,'" said Jake as he bowed ostentatiously, arms outstretched in a mocking show of reverence. "Please, Master, lead me to the fount of innovation knowledge."

Finbarr enjoyed the caricature and responded in character. "My child, it will not be easy. You will travel many difficult roads seeking wisdom; you will walk the foothills for long periods looking for inspiration. But if you read the entrails, if you study the signs, you may indeed find the path to wisdom and innovation. Then, you can reach the mountain top and see the world clearly."

"Gosh, this should be good. Master, I am in your hands."

"You are welcome, my friend. Now let's get back to reality. You heard of Evel Knievel?"

"The stunt motorcyclist? Sure have. Grew up watching a lot of television programming about him. Dreamed I would be like him some day. You know, jumping a motor-bike across the Grand Canyon or some other lunatic escapade."

"I think at one stage, most kids—well boys— dreamed of being Evel Knievel. But even if you can't be him, you can learn from him."

"You're losing me again. Are we still talking innovation?"

"We are. Go back to your Grand Canyon example for a moment. If Evel planned to jump the canyon and had only finite resources, which of these options do you think he might have gone for: option A - Load the bike up with as much rocket fuel as possible and really go for it in one effort or, option B - Just put a little fuel into the bike, plan to do a number of different jumps and hope one of them might succeed?"

"Well, he'd be crazy to try the latter option, wouldn't he? The chances of success are limited no matter what, but his best option is to go gangbuster for it, and really try and make it happen. Have I given the correct answer, Master?"

"Yes, my child, but the logic you expounded there, does not apply to the innovation process in many organizations."

"What do you mean?"

"Well, for many companies, there is a set innovation budget—one tank of rocket fuel if you like, which is then divided out to satisfy all the various product launches during the fiscal period. The result is, that many of the efforts to jump across that metaphorical Grand Canyon are completely under-resourced. There is not enough fuel in the tank and what happens? Failure. The chances of jumping the Grand Canyon are slim in any event, but when you do not put sufficient fuel in that tank, you might as well be 'Blowin' in the wind'—Bob Dylan-like, you know."

"Yeah, I get it. Got to say I like your reference to trekking the foothills, Finbarr. When I go back Stateside, I'll work with my team to trek those foothills. I mean, we'll definitely spend more time in-store, watching, observing and also asking plenty of those dumb questions that you talk about."

"It will be time well spent, Jake. Keep your customers involved all the time."

"I agree with that, Finbarr. Doesn't always happen though. Buddy of mine works for a Blue Chip company back home. Met him recently. You know when someone is really frustrated with something?"

"Yeah, I know the feeling. Been there, done that."

"Well, he was furious about the waste of money on a recent innovation program. One of their consultant teams persuaded the global marketing chief to fly in senior management for a one day innovation think-tank in Denver, Colorado. About twenty senior execs flew in from Europe, Latin America, Asia, to brainstorm for one day. The thing that really annoyed him is—no customers were involved and many of the execs would only have met their respective customers at negotiating sessions or social functions. But, hey—these were the guys in charge. The session was a waste of time. Executives who did not walk in the customers' shoes trying to develop solutions for problems they did not fully understand or even knew existed."

Finbarr nodded, "And you can be sure, that was not the end of it. I bet project teams were set up to follow through on the favored options, which of course required additional meetings, and more directives from senior management to subordinates, to validate the concepts.

"In all fairness, it is great to be the hurler on the ditch though, isn't it?"

"Master, I am lost again," said a bemused Jake.

"It's an Irish saying, Jake. Hurling is one of our national sports—fifteen big strapping lads beating a ball the size of a baseball around a field with hurley sticks. You guys would probably call them wooden clubs. Anyway, the hurler on the ditch is the guy who just sits there watching the world go by, criticizing everyone, finding fault with the world, but never providing solutions."

"I see what you mean. Do you want to get off the ditch?"

"Maybe so. I might get a thorn in my butt if I sit on the ditch too long. I shall now come down from the ditch and provide you with 'The Holy Grail of Innovation.'"

"This should be good."

"'The Holy Grail of Innovation' is provided by VIP products. Let me explain. VIP products generate three things. Incremental Volume that's the 'V,' incremental Image—'I' for image, and finally 'P,' incremental Profits. The companies that create those VIP elements—incremental Volume, Image, Profit are successful. Jake, they are few and far between, but you should study them and understand how the VIP products have been generated and why they are successful."

"I like the concept, Finbarr. How about some examples, Guru?"

"Do you eat in McDonald's?"

"More often than I used to. I like their salads—that has been a great addition to their menu."

"Spot on. VIP products, Jake. Those salads have generated incremental *volume* for the chain, salads have improved the overall *image* of the McDonald's brand and of course salads have generated the P—incremental profitability. Those are true VIP products. The McDonald's success also shatters a couple of myths."

"It does?"

"At least two. Salads have been a massive success for McDonald's, even though the chain was not the first to introduce quality salads into the fast food market. Indeed, McDonald's *Premium Salads* were introduced almost a year after Wendy's introduced their *Garden Sensation Salads*. Being first to market is of course important, but not always critical. The other myth is that new products must be innovative.

"Think about this, Jake. How stupid is it, how ironic is it, that *the* most successful new product introduced by the hamburger chains in a generation, is something as basic as lettuce?"

"Never thought of it that way, Finbarr, but you have a point. If I had said three years ago, 'I'm going to McDonald's or Wendy's for a salad,' I think someone would have called for the men in white coats to take me away. Mind you, McDonald's did have *Salad Shakers* for a few years which were not really successful. The difference is, the new salads—from all the chains, Finbarr, are good. In fact, it is a quality that would be acceptable in a mid-scale restaurant."

"Wow, Jake, that's a change in perception."

"Maybe. The market back home was also ready for these new salads. Consumers were tired of burgers, fries and the lack of variety on the menu and there was a momentum towards healthy products— or at least perceived healthy products."

"Jake, your wisdom grows in direct correlation to the time you spend breathing the beautiful Irish fresh air and of course, consuming copious pints of that 'Black Magic' we call Guinness."

Jake felt his wisdom grew in direct correlation to the time spent with his cousin, but he did not wish to build Finbarr's ego.

"Thank you, 'O Great and Wise One.' You know McDonald's did something else you referenced previously. It advertised salads aggressively and continued with that investment. McDonald's didn't do the 'Lemmy' thing. It focused and stayed focused. I reckon everyone in the target market was aware of the product launch. The hype around it was amazing. You're right, Finbarr. It is crazy a hamburger chain invests so much on salads. But, it is getting results. It's a funny old world."

"That's right. That's right."

"Do you remember the old TV commercials,

Finbarr, when every ad seemed to proclaim, 'New and improved?'"

"Ah, we didn't have TV in those days, Jake. Every evening we would go dancing at the crossroads and have impure thoughts about chaste Irish colleens. That was only the boys though, I'll have you know. We didn't know in those days, that the chaste Irish colleens might also be having impure thoughts."

"I think you can get down from your Irish image horse now, Finbarr. It's me you are talking to."

Finbarr smiled and mimicked a thick brogue, similar to that he exhibited for the American visitors at the gas station. "Ah begorrah, now sir, 'tis true sir. So it is. To be sure, I remember when the first television set came to the village. Oh, there was fierce excitement and commotion altogether. Fierce altogether, now. I'm tellin' ya. We would all crowd into Moriarty's Pub to see The Angelus broadcast at six o'clock. It was just a still graphic of the The Blessed Virgin in grainy black and white and people would come for miles around to see it. If the reception was really bad, sir, wouldn't they be tellin' the tallest kid in the parish to stand on the thatched roof of Moriarty's Pub and hold the TV antenna higher. Ah, them was the days, when every kitchen had a framed montage of The Pope and JFK. You'd pray that the sainted, good living, ever-faithful Irish Catholic President Kennedy would save us from the evils of communism and all the Irish mothers wished their marriage was as happy as Kennedy's."

"A good brand image creates its own reality, Finbarr, and you know that better than anyone."

Dropping the exaggerated brogue, Finbarr continued, now laughing in unison with Jake. "You know, we have two regulars down at the pub who make a nice living spinning yarns like that last one, to gullible people. One guy, Sean Hannity, loves to blarney any audience who will listen. Not much of it is accurate of course, but people want to believe. As a result, he makes great tips or as you Yanks might say, 'grah-two-e-teees.' The other guy, Moore, is just as good at BS-ing his audience."

"His first name wouldn't be 'Michael,' would it, Finbarr?"

"Actually, it is. Michael Moore. How'd you know that?" queried Finbarr with a straight face.

"Oh, just a guess. Just a guess."

Before Jake could comment further, Finbarr continued. "Guys like Sean Hannity and Michael Moore are what we call 'seanchais.' Seanchais were the first type of mass media in Ireland if you will. They were story tellers who wound part fact, part fiction, part aspiration into whatever message they wished to communicate. Those who wanted to believe—believed. When the two seanchais down at the pub get going, we sometimes refer to them as the Hannity and Moore Show. These guys know how to create a message and communicate to a responsive target audience."

"Finbarr, I wasn't sure if there was method to your madness when I met you first. I'm back in that spot again."

Finbarr had a mischievous look on his face. "Don't know what you are talking about there, Yank. It was you who brought up advertising and new improved products? All I'm saying is, the challenge facing you and other innovators is to find ways to communicate your product message effectively to your target audience."

"Of course. You couldn't possibly mean anything else," Jake said, shaking his head in puzzled wonderment. "Any more VIP products? Remember, that is where this conversation started."

"You've a great memory there, Jake. VIP, VIP... I'm sure you can think of a few, but others include Apple's iPod and I think JetBlue would qualify in this category."

"Agree with you on the iPod, Finbarr. Very VIP.

Huge volumes—over two million sold in a recent quarter. Apple's image as an innovative company is reinforced by this product launch and, of course, incremental profits are being generated."

"Couldn't have said it better myself, Jake. The same kind of logic applies to JetBlue. Its volumes are incredible. Those guys fill almost ninety percent of seats. JetBlue most definitely has built a great image for itself and changed travelers' expectations of what an airline can do, and guess what. JetBlue is the most profitable airline in margin terms in the U.S. Volume. Image. Profit, again. VIP products are successful because they strike a chord with their target market. Give your customers what they want, in a better format than others and you can succeed."

"I believe you, Finbarr. I now better appreciate that Toyota concept you mentioned the other day—what did you call it again?"

"Genchi Genbutsu—'Go to the source and learn.' Toyota did it with their Toyota brand and they most certainly did it with Lexus."

"My tax advisor drives a Lexus, Finbarr. He raves about it. It's a great car, never any problems. The amazing thing is that it was only introduced in nineteen eighty-nine. Now it's the best-selling luxury marque back home."

"That's right. That's right. Here, we had a Japanese company, known for reliable vehicles—the Toyota brand, creating a luxury product to take on the likes of Mercedes-Benz, BMW and Cadillac. The industry thought Toyota was crazy, until the Lexus was seen by the public."

"So how did they do it?"

"Genchi Genbutsu, Jake, Genchi Genbutsu. The head honcho in Toyota America, a guy called ... let me think, let me think ...Yukiyasu Togo ..."

"Doubt if he was Irish."

"No, just as smart though. Togo told his designers and engineers to immerse themselves in American culture. After all, the car was being developed for the American market. This guy told his team they could not create what he called 'A child of America' unless they understood Americans."

Jake repeated slowly, " 'A child of America.' Where do you learn all this stuff, Finbarr?"

"I dunno. Maybe it is an Irish form of Genchi Genbutsu. I suppose it should be called 'Genchi O'Genbutsu.' We could call it 'GoG' for short. But you can do it, you can 'GoG' as well, Jake—read, understand, go to the source, learn, and implement."

"I know. Walk those supermarket aisles, observe a lot by watching, and ask dumb questions."

"Be careful though. Don't just study your industry when looking for successes and trends."

"You mean I should follow the advice of all those consultants and think out of the box. Yeah?"

"Never said a truer word, Jake. The Lexus team studied more than their industry. They set themselves up in some classy spot in California. Some place called Laguna Beach."

"That would be right. It's a high income area."

"That's the reason they went there. Lexus studied how affluent Americans lived, what they did to enjoy themselves, how they spent money on luxury items, what turned them on—all that jazz. And then, they took all that knowledge—the tactile appreciation if you will, combined it with great engineering and *voila!* or whatever the Japanese word is, a world-class luxury car that took the industry by storm. And they are still doing it. You know their sports car model?"

"The SC 430. That is a beaut! Now there's my dream car."

"Not a bad dream to have, Jake. When designing that model, the poor deprived Lexus designers didn't get to go to Laguna Beach at all. This time the unfortunate guys were sent to the South of France to study luxury, admire classic art and architecture and gain inspiration to create a beautiful car."

"Some people have it tough, Finbarr. And you know something, it's going to be tough for me, if we don't eat soon. Can we talk about this over food?"

"I'm all for that. We'll go down to the pub."

"You've a good menu down there. It's Irish Stew for me."

"Whatever you feel like. Me? I'm going to have Tikka Masala. Would you ever think the most popular dish in Jack McCarthy's Bar—among Irish people, like—would be a dish called Tikka Masala? We do a Winter Special, Tikka Masala and a pint. Flies out the door it does. You wanna walk down?"

Chapter Nine

The Black Belt Cop

---- ♣ ----

Lesson:
The Brand Image

---- ♣ ----

I think Ms. (Marilyn) Monroe's architecture is extremely good architecture.

—Frank Lloyd Wright

Approaching the pub, Finbarr elbowed Jake playfully in the ribs. "Hey, hey, Jake. Look what we got here. The love of your life—Fiona, and your opposition."

Sitting on a bench outside Jack McCarthy's Bar, Jake saw Fiona and a fit looking man holding hands. A coffee cup in front of both.

"Is it the love-birds I see in front of me?" said Finbarr.

"Ah, Finbarr, how are ya? Jake, howz it go-ann?" said a smiling, animated Fiona. "Gerry, have you met Finbarr's Yankee cousin?—Jake."

Gerry rose slowly from the bench, straightening with some obvious difficulty.

"Jake, great to meet you. Fiona was telling me she met you. Hope Finbarr isn't leading you astray.

Well not too much, I mean."

"Gerry, I think I'm becoming a willing stray. That's the problem."

Finbarr looked quizzically at Gerry. "You look like a guy in trouble there. Did Fiona hit you a wallop or what?"

"If only. Naw, I had a spot of bother with a few kids from the next parish, last night. Four of them were vandalizing the school and I had to take them on before I got some backup. One guy hit me in the ribs with something. It's not too bad. The doc gave me a few painkillers, which is why I'm drinkin' coffee. God, I'd give anything for a pint."

"So, was there a big scrap then?" said Finbarr.

"Not really. One of the gurriers recognized me. I had a run in with him before. He shouted something like, 'It's the black belt cop,' and they all just froze. They all gave in."

"Gerry, I haven't been in this village very long, but everyone seems to know you as 'the black belt cop.'"

"That's right, Jake. Finbarr gives me some of his marketing blarney and tells me it's my brand image. Did you ever hear anything so dumb?"

Finbarr interjected. "Gerry, if you had brains, you'd be dangerous. 'The black belt cop' *is* your brand image. You benefit from it. Do you think those guys would have gone so quietly last night if they didn't know about your black belt?"

O'Regan had now straightened to his full height. To the six-foot-tall Jake's surprise, Gerry was only at his eye-level.

"Ah, will ya whist?" said a now embarrassed Gerry. "How can a brand image make you bigger? Those guys were just young pups who had no bottle."

"Gerry, you can believe what you want, but the more gurriers around here who know you as 'the black belt cop,' the easier your job will be. Keep that brand image. We'll let Hollywood know about you, and they might do a TV series called *The Black Belt Cop*. The only trouble is, you'd be too ugly to appear in it. Maybe Jake here could play the part. Fiona could still be the girlfriend though."

Finbarr smiled and winked at his cousin.

"Gerry, can you arrest people here in Ireland for BS?" quipped Jake. "Finbarr could be given a life sentence."

"Naw, the rest of the prisoners would complain. If they were stuck with him, they'd moan about cruel and unusual punishment. They'd start some organization like 'Irish Prisoners for Justice.' Why don't you just take him back to the States with you?"

"That mightn't be a bad idea."

Finbarr nodded to Jake. "O.K., we'll leave you love-birds. Fiona, be gentle with him, will ya?"

"I'll do that, Finbarr. I won't use the handcuffs tonight."

"C'mon, Jake. It's time to go. You'll be having impure thoughts here. See you guys around."

As they walked away from the young couple, Gerry O'Regan shouted, "Hey, Finbarr. Got a phone call from a buddy—Dave Murphy. He tells me you've got married. Must have been a quiet wedding."

Finbarr kept walking but smiled, clenched his right hand behind his back and extended his middle finger in Gerry's direction.

Chapter Ten

The ER Factor

--- ♣ ---

Lesson:
Drivers of Corporate Health

--- ♣ ---

"You can't have a clean floor with a dirty mop bucket. To be successful you need to take care of the basics of your business— and that means making sure you don't overlook the little details."

—Dave Thomas,
    Wendy's International, Inc.

The crowing cock did its work. Jake awoke and lay on the bed for a few minutes. With mixed emotions, he anticipated his final day in Ireland. He was anxious to return home, now newly energized to attack his problem business. He had grown to love this country in one very short week. He had also grown to love his Irish cousin and the wisdom he espoused.

The loud music in the kitchen alerted Jake to Finbarr's presence. Finbarr was singing along to U2's "It's a Beautiful Day."

"Morning, Jake. Thought I'd give you a bit of Irish culture on your last day. Bono and the boys. We got the weather to go with the song as well."

"At least I can listen to their music. That Bono guy is a good man in every sense of the word. He's done a lot to raise awareness of the AIDS crisis in Africa."

"That's right. That's right. He toured Africa in 2002 with then Treasury Secretary Paul O'Neill and apparently knew as much about the problem as O'Neill did."

"He's a 'GoG' guy."

"Huh! I know U2 is big in Japan, Jake, but that doesn't make Bono a 'GoG,' does it?"

"I'm serious. Bono was interviewed on one of our cable news shows just before I flew over. He was interviewed by Bill O'Reilly—does a program called *The O'Reilly Factor*. Bono had done a number of speaking engagements in the States to raise the profile of AIDS and Third World debt. Before he did the engagements, he read the Declaration of Independence and he read the U.S. Constitution so he could better relate to his audiences and craft a message that was truly relevant for them."

"Wow, that is impressive—he really did go to the source to try and understand, but it just shows, 'GoG' is relevant for many, many situations."

"Even for rock stars doing God's work. That's what O'Reilly told him—that he was doing 'God's work.' He could also have said he was doing the work of 'GoG.'"

"Very PP there again, Jake. Now before we save the Third World, let's make sure we solve your crisis first. Are we going to see your ugly mug back here some time soon?"

"You try and keep me away, Finbarr."

"That's the spirit; I can always use another barman during the summer season, although hopefully, *JB's Good Food* will be doing so well you will not need to double-job."

"I believe I can turn it around, Finbarr, and it's thanks to you. I owe you one. I really owe you."

"Ah will ya get outta here. I haven't told you anything new. You just needed a break to refresh your dream. Find your 'desert highway' and you'll be well on your way to success."

" 'Desert highway?' What do you mean?"

Finbarr commenced singing in a very out of tune manner, "*Somewhere on a desert highway, she rides a Harley-Davidson. Her long blonde hair flyin' in the wind.* Remember the Neil Young line from the song 'Unknown Legend'? It's the imagery and vision. You clarify your vision, your 'desert highway' like, and then all you have to worry about is the *ER Factor— Drivers of Corporate Health.*"

"Completely agree with you, Finbarr. That 'ER Factor' is just the missing piece in the puzzle. Don't know why it isn't used more often to be honest with you. In fact ..."

"So you know about the 'ER Factor' then?"

"'ER Factor'? I haven't a clue what you're talking about, but it's nice to string you along."

"You've been in Ireland too long, Jake. I think I'll take you to the airport early today. Wouldn't want you to miss the plane and get further contaminated by the Irish mindset. Anyway...The 'ER Factor' stands for E - Execution, of an R - Relevant strategy. The company that can execute a strategy that is relevant for its market will succeed. Thus the ER Factor is a Driver of Corporate Health."

"Nice concept, Finbarr. Some of the companies you spoke about earlier in the week are good examples of executing against a relevant strategy. JetBlue, Starbucks, Ryanair probably fall into that category."

"That's right. That's right. But the best example of how the 'ER Factor' works is the world's favorite burger place—McDonald's. What those guys have done to resurrect the business in such a short time is —what would you Yanks say?—'Awesome, dude. Awesome.'"

"Yeah, they've done a pretty good turnaround job alright. And you think this 'ER Factor' is the reason?"

"I reckon it's a major contributor. Look, prior to

those two dudes—Cantalupo and Bell taking over, that company was struggling big time."

"It's sad about Cantalupo. He fulfilled his life's dream to become Chairman, and fifteen, sixteen months later he's dead. Life is strange."

"Aye, Jake, but I bet when Chairman Cantalupo went to that great hamburger restaurant in the sky, the Great Maitre d' said, 'You done a good job, man.' And he did, Jake. You know McDonald's is a poster child for proving both sides of the 'ER Factor.' "

"If you say so."

"As John Wayne might have said, 'Shure do, Pardner. I shure do.' There are a lot of theories as to why McDonald's struggled for years, but think about this. Between 1996 and 2000, the Chairman's Letter in the Corporation's Annual Report referenced the 'customer experience' once. Can you believe it? Just once in five reports. Isn't that amazing? This, from an organization whose vision was to be 'The world's best quick-service restaurant experience.' The organization spent so much time on building out new restaurants, it forgot to look after its core market—its current customers—and satisfy them."

"You mean it is like that car you complained about when you drove me from the airport. Going somewhere, but unaware of the surroundings."

"That's the perfect example, but as it became more obvious that McDonald's results were not satisfactory, attitudes and objectives changed. They had to."

An animated Finbarr was now warming to his topic.

"Get this, Jake. The 2001 annual report was published in March 2002 and showed a dramatic change. Then Chairman, Jack Greenberg said, 'First and foremost, we plan to improve the customers' experience ... We have rededicated ourselves to giving customers ... an outstanding experience.'"

"He came to that viewpoint a little late, I reckon," Jake opined.

"Guess so, although the current organization will benefit ultimately from the huge build-out of restaurants he was responsible for. My point though is when McDonald's lost sight of the customer, when they did not execute properly, when their strategy was not relevant for their core, they lost customers, their image started to fade and of course profitability was impacted."

"The Golden Arches were tarnished alright, Finbarr. Kind of a negative VIP—negative volume, negative image, negative profit."

"That's right. That's right. The arches sure needed a bit of spit and polish, and the new management appreciated that pretty fast. I remember cranking up my computer and listening to Cantalupo's first conference call with analysts, following his appointment as Chairman. One comment he made really stuck with me—'Clean restrooms in every restaurant and hot fresh food served quickly in every restaurant would be a change.'"

"The Chairman of McDonald's said that!"

"He did indeed. January sixteen, two thousand and three. It was such a mind-blowing comment, the date is burned into my brain. Cantalupo realized the company had to get back to basics. Fast. I'll tell you something. A friend of mine, Mick Barry runs a very successful restaurant, a few miles from here. He doesn't spend a cent on advertising, but spends his time on what he calls 'Toilet Marketing.'"

Jake gave Finbarr a wry look. "What in God's name is 'Toilet Marketing?'"

"It's getting the basics right, Jake. Mick claims that the element that will make the biggest impression on his restaurant customers—even more than the food—is the quality of his toilets or restrooms, as you call them."

Jake looked with respect at Finbarr and said slowly, "Oh my God, I now believe you are a genius."

"Only *now* you believe it?" responded Finbarr,

feigning hurt. "What has convinced you?"

"You—'Toilet Marketing.' I was at a Lexus gig a few weeks ago, back home. The company is doing promotional road-shows in some of the big cities. Lexus drivers and potential drivers get invited to test-drive Lexus vehicles and competitors—you know, Mercedes, BMW, Cadillac and the like at a specially laid out track. It is a really well organized gig, but do you know what impressed me most on the day?"

"What?"

"The restrooms. I swear, Finbarr. What you are saying makes so much sense. All the cars, Lexus and competitors were good, but you expect that. But at one point, I went to the restrooms. These were the portable type, where you expect just the basics. I went into the restrooms and thought, *Wow*. They looked like the best quality restrooms you'd find in the most upscale country club. Admittedly, it was a faux finish, but the overall effect was really, really classy. Lexus likes to talk about the 'Pursuit of Excellence.' It doesn't just relate to their cars. It's everything they do with, and for their customers, which is of course, one of the reasons the brand image is so strong."

"Well, well, well. Isn't that amazing? The thing that impressed you most during a day testing luxury cars is the can, sorry restrooms. But it's just one more example of the ER Factor.

"McDonald's is now using the same logic. Charlie Bell, the Aussie guy who took over the CEO role when Cantalupo departed, consistently stated McDonald's would have the cleanest restrooms in the industry. Isn't that daft? At investor conferences, prior to his resignation due to ill health, Bell regularly made that statement. He wished to get across the message that consumers go to restaurants for food, but they will boycott restaurants that get the basics wrong, such as toilets."

"You're not saying though that clean restrooms is the reason for their recovery. There is more to it than that."

"You're right. But the restrooms are a symptom of the overall effect—the emphasis on execution. The relevant strategy that those burger gurus developed, is to get more customers into current restaurants and focus on that. Contrast that with the previous strategy of more customers via more restaurants and then failing to execute the in-store experience properly. In retrospect, it is easy to see which is better for corporate health."

"I get it. Develop the relevant strategy and execute well against it. Seems to have worked for

McDonald's alright."

"That's an understatement. Jake, do you know how you build great results? Get the simple things, the basics right. You've seen the positive press McDonald's received, but did you know more than two million extra customers are visiting their restaurants today in the United States, compared to twelve—fourteen months ago."

"Two million more ... a day?" Jake said disbelievingly.

"That's right. That's right. More than two million additional people every day. The ironic thing is McDonald's claims this is the equivalent of building more than 1,500 new restaurants."

"Wow! The 'ER Factor!'"

"When thinking about your business, you need to know, you need to be certain, Jake, what the ethical success factors are, which you must execute against. Everyone in your company must know those also. That is one of the reasons McDonald's has turned around so fast."

"Clear metrics—makes sense."

"That's right. That's right. Jake, how come you Yanks use 'metrics' when you don't use the metric system? Shouldn't you guys say 'yardics?'"

"Let's debate that some other day, Finbarr."

"Agreed. Anyway, McDonald's set out clear metrics for restaurant and personnel performance across a range of areas. If those metrics were not met, the responsible executives got a metaphorical whack across the head from one of the boomerangs Charlie Bell brought from Australia."

"Do you know what turned me away from McDonald's a few years back, Finbarr? It was those things that Cantalupo and Bell complained about, but the biggest turn off for me was their advertising. They ran a campaign that said 'Smile,' or 'We love to see you smile.' But what happened when you went into a McDonald's restaurant? Your server was like Mr. Grumps on a bad day. I think it was David Feherty, the sports commentator, who said about golfer Colin Montgomery: 'He sometimes looks like a bulldog who has bitten a nettle.' That's what the experience was like when you asked for a Big Mac."

"Good ol' 'Monty.' Whips you guys in the Ryder Cup every time."

"Unfortunately. He sure does know how to execute when it comes to the Ryder Cup."

"That 'smile' example, Jake, is a great one. The marketing guys in an organization dream up a campaign, but the implications of it are not properly understood or driven through. Failure to execute will cripple you. Ha! Don't mean to be politically incorrect but let's go back to 'Mighty Mick' O'Leary and Ryanair again. Ryanair is another poster child for the 'ER Factor.' It is so focused on executing against a relevant strategy—low cost, low cost, low cost, that it was sued in a UK court recently because it forced a disabled passenger to pay an £18 fee for use of a wheelchair."

Jake looked wide-eyed at Finbarr. "You've got to be joking, Finbarr."

"I am not," Finbarr responded firmly. "The Ryanair view is that its job is to fly people from point to point and that the airport authorities' role is to provide facilities to get the passengers on the plane."

Jake looked at Finbarr in astonishment. "They went to court to defend *not* providing a wheelchair for one of their passengers. They're crazy."

"No, Jake. They're not crazy; they are just manic about Executing against a Relevant strategy—low cost. There's no flies on O'Leary, I tell ya, and if there was, they'd be renting space, so they would.

"This particular passenger walked with the aid of crutches, but felt the distance to the gate was too much for him. When he requested a wheelchair to take him to his departure gate, Ryanair directed him to a third-party services provider who charged him

£18. The guy sued Ryanair for not providing wheel-chair facilities for the disabled. Ryanair claims that more than eighty of the airports it flies into provide wheelchair facilities at the airport authority's expense and it sees no reason why airlines should provide the wheelchair facility."

"That might be so Finbarr, but the airline is being petty. Not to mind it must have been a disaster from a PR point of view."

"If the objective is to be *the* low-cost airline, nothing gets in their way. I think their logic is sound, but not many companies would have been prepared to take the PR fallout from an event like this. But the bottom line is this: Ryanair will do everything possible to keep costs down, and then they combine it with superb execution. It is fascinating to see how fast they can unload and load a plane—the twenty-five minute target. Jake, the next time you are at an airport, compare the speed a low-cost carrier like Southwest turns a plane around compared to United, American or one of the other big airlines. Southwest and Ryanair know turnaround is critical for success. For Ryanair, the never-ending emphasis on the ER Factor has provided amazing results. Not only is it the most profitable airline in Europe, it is number one in punctuality and has the lowest rate of lost bags in the industry."

"Geez, Finbarr, I'd fly them just for that reason. I seem to lose a bag every other flight in the States."

"Yeah, it can be a pain in the butt alright, but according to Ryanair, six bags are misplaced per ten thousand passengers. One of the reasons for this number of course, is because it flies to out-of-the-way airports where bags will not get misplaced so easily. It also flies point-to-point and does not use a hub and spoke type system that you guys love over there in America. All of these individual execution points contribute to the airline having the lowest breakeven rate per plane in the industry—a passenger load factor of fifty-nine percent. When you compare that to Ryanair's actual load factor of eighty-one percent, you can see why it makes money. The airline flies almost half-a-million more passengers than BA does, *per month.* Can you believe it?"

"Finbarr, seems like the only thing Ryanair is missing is the fish and chips we had in Mick's Plaice the other night. Ryanair could use the slogan 'Great Flights—Great Food,' but that wouldn't be executing against a relevant strategy, would it?"

"That's right. That's right. It would not be using the 'ER Factor' to drive corporate health."

"Finbarr, if I had too much of those fish and chips

it mightn't be too good for personal health either. What if Ryanair stuck with their current policy and used the copy line, 'Nothing fishy about our flights?' "

"Jake, you need to go home—soon," intoned a smiling Finbarr. "I knew we'd have you talking funny. Now you're thinking funny as well. Although now that you mention Mick's Plaice, his business is a prime example of the 'ER Factor.' Doubt if he knows it, though. He has been asked to expand his menu to do some fancy things like wraps and cheese poppers, but the guy says 'No Way.' He has lines outside the door every night, because he gives his customers what they want—the best fish and chips. Do you remember the sign you commented on the night we were down there, or do you remember anything from that night?"

Jake looked blankly at Finbarr. "I just have this vague memory of good fresh fish, but I don't remember much else from that gourmet establishment."

"Gourmet establishment!" Finbarr grinned. "Mick will like that reference, so he will. He has a sign on his window that reads 'Mick's Fish 'n' Chips—World famous in the County.' "

"That's good Irish logic for you, Finbarr. 'World famous in the County.' It's not logical, but it makes sense."

"You got it, Jake. See, you are thinking like an Irishman."

"I'll need some more time here to become a true convert. I know what you say makes sense, but it is not easy to make your 'ER Factor' work."

"Of course, it is not easy—otherwise everyone would be doing it."

"If they thought of it, Finbarr."

"On the button again, Jake. The first thing you have to do, and I mean *you*, is: decide to do it. Decide to do it, Jake. Then understand what is required to *Execute* against a *Relevant* strategy.

"If you study your customers' needs properly, you have a chance, and realistically, maybe that is all it is—a chance—to develop a better strategy which you can execute against. Go back to JetBlue again. Before it came on the scene, not many people would have believed you could improve on the very successful Southwest model. No one believed it except the founder of JetBlue—David Neeleman and some of his colleagues."

"Did you know he was fired by Southwest after less than six months?"

"*Who?*" said a surprised Finbarr. "Neeleman was fired by Southwest? Well, you learn something new every day."

♣

"They didn't fire him for incompetence or anything. From what I remember, he was part of Morris
Air, another airline he started, which was purchased
by Southwest. Southwest just found him to be too
impetuous for their company and asked him to leave."

"Any lesson you can take out of that, Jake?"

"Yeah, don't fire guys just because they are
mavericks and don't conform to your culture."

Finbarr nodded. "You're looking for miracles if
you want that to happen. Very few people will survive
when they don't fit a culture, but there is an even
bigger lesson for you, Mr. 'Soon to be successful
entrepreneur.' It is this. No one, Jake, *no one* goes
through life without some pain, some disappointment
or failures. Neeleman, you say, was fired by
Southwest. Others have suffered the same fate. Do
you know that the father of mass-transportation,
Henry Ford himself, was fired within a week of taking
his first job in Detroit, and look at the McDonald's
guy—Jim Cantalupo. He left the company, left it,
Jake, eight months before he was asked to return as
Chairman. Cantalupo probably never thought he
would make it to Chairman, but he overcame the
disappointment of leaving the company to return
and bring it back to glory. You know he probably had
that Nixon experience you referenced earlier in the

week. The time out of the business helped him understand the issues in a clearer light."

"Finbarr, Ernest Hemmingway said it best in *A Farewell to Arms* when he wrote, 'The world breaks everyone and afterward many are strong at the broken place.'"

"That's right. That's right. You learn more from problems and failures than you do from success."

Jake nodded, taking Finbarr's comments to heart.

"Jake, I'm going to do a 'Yogi Berra' on you. 'When you see a fork in the road, take it.' I want to take a fork back to JetBlue. It looked at how it could improve on the Southwest model, and you know what? It has. JetBlue introduced newer and, it claims, more comfortable planes. The A320 Airbus is a slightly wider plane than the Boeing equivalent. On board, it executes exceptionally well."

"And JetBlue has a policy to not overbook apparently."

"That's right. That's right. The net result, Jake, is that it has won the best domestic airline award two years running, and ninety-four percent of their customers state the JetBlue experience is either somewhat better or much better than other airlines."

"That can't be right, Finbarr. No one gets those ratings in surveys. You're telling me that almost

♣

every one of their customers believes JetBlue is better than any other airline!"

"That's what their research says. It should go into *Ripley's Believe It or Not*. It is almost incredible and you know what the ultimate result is?—Profit, man. Good profits. In margin terms, JetBlue is the most profitable airline in the U.S. Now there's a paradox for you. The most profitable, fastest growing airline with the highest customer satisfaction rating is a low fare airline."

"The 'ER Factor' again."

"Based on a very clear vision. The success of JetBlue stems from Neeleman's belief and vision in bringing humanity back to the airways. After that it was just a walk in the park," said a smiling Finbarr. "Jake, I'm tellin' you. You can do it too. You can do it."

"I believe you, Finbarr. I really do believe you."

"C'mon, let's get out of here. We've got to get you to the airport."

"O.K.," said a resigned Jake. "It's been fun. It's been a lot of fun."

On the journey to the airport, the cousins regaled each other with memories of a week both thoroughly enjoyed. The recent speeding fine had not impacted Finbarr's driving performance. Jake did muse to himself that he no longer felt uncomfortable with the Irishman's driving.

Finbarr stopped the car outside Departures two hours before Jake's flight. The two cousins and now good friends exited the car.

"I'll leave you here, Jake. No point in hanging around inside."

"That's fine, Finbarr. I don't know how to thank you. You've got to come over some time and build a business Stateside."

"Don't know about that, Jake. I'd be a bit like General Paddy—except I wouldn't be able to feed all the customers."

"Finbarr. You would find a way. You've got a gift. Not just business-wise, but in making people feel good. Right now, I feel as if I could dance on mushrooms."

Finbarr looked him in the eye. "Jake, you will dance on mushrooms. Leprechauns dance on mushrooms when they feel good and believe they can change the world. You are going to change your world, Mr. 'Soon to be successful entrepreneur.' Believe it, Jake, believe it and you will dance on mushrooms."

The two friends hugged.

Releasing each other, Jake held Finbarr at both shoulders. "Finbarr, you should write a book on all the things you have told me."

"Will ya cut the blarney and get on your plane. I suppose you've got a title for it as well, have ya?"

"Yes, I do. Use the General Hank and General Paddy story. Title it, *Why Ireland Never Invaded America*."

Finbarr waved his cousin a fond goodbye.

"Get on your plane. *Why Ireland Never Invaded America*. Who in their right mind would buy a book with that title?"

NOTES

Chapter 1

P. 13 "When You Wrapped":
http://clubtread.com/sforum/topic.asp?TOPIC_ID=1781,
referenced on this and several other web sites as "Worst
country song titles." November, 2004.

P. 13 Tom Peters and Bob Waterman, *In Search of Excellence:
Lessons from America's Best Run Companies* (Harper &
Row, New York, 1982).

P. 14 "Was Kmart": *In Search of Excellence: Lessons from
Americas Best Run Companies*, Ibid., p.21.

Chapter 2

P. 24 *Special K* is a registered trademark of Kellogg's Corporation.

P. 30 "(H)umanity back to air travel": Chairman's Letter,
JetBlue Annual Report, 2002.

P. 31 "(Y)ou'll enjoy": First cited (to author) by Irish
Supermarket guru, Feargal Quinn, Founder Superquinn,
about twenty years ago. He was referencing Delta
Airlines (then considered a "model" airline).

P. 33 Embraer: JetBlue press release, 6/10/2003.

P. 37 "I will build": Sidney Olsen, *Young Henry Ford: A Picture
History of the First Forty Years* (reprint, Detroit, Mich.,
Wayne State University Press, 1997), p.182.

P. 39 "The idea of Disney": Bob Thomas, *Walt Disney — An
American Original* (Simon & Schuster, New York, 1976),
p.246.

P. 41 "In the hill country": Joseph A. Califano, *The Triumph &
Tragedy of Lyndon — The White House Years* (Simon &
Schuster, New York, 1991) p.58.

Chapter 3

P. 54 "Beer for my Horses": Toby Keith/Scotty Emerick,
Unleashed (Music-CD—Dreamworks, Nashville, 2002).

P. 60 "The third place": Commonly cited by Ray Oldenburg,
*The Great Good Place: Cafes, Coffee Shops, Community
Centers, Beauty Parlors, General Stores, Bars, Hangouts and
How They Get You Through the Day* (Paragon House,
New York, 1989).

P. 63   Outback Steakhouse Management Presentation, at
        CIBC Conference, online 7/8/2003.

Chapter 5

P. 84   "Dodge Hotel": Robert Dallek, *Lone Star Rising—Lyndon
        Johnson and His Times, 1908-1960* (Oxford University
        Press, 1991), p.96.

P. 86   *Big Mac* is a registered trademark of McDonald's
        Corporation.

P. 87   *Garden Sensation* is a registered trademark of Wendy's Inc.

Chapter 6

P. 96   "All men dream": T.E. Lawrence, *Seven Pillars of
        Wisdom: A Triumph,* (Anchor Books, New York, 1926) p. 24.

Chapter 7

P. 107 "Everything can be taken": Viktor Emil Frankel, *Man's
        Search for Meaning,* (Pocket Books, New York, 1959) p. 86.

P. 107 "We who lived": ibid., p86.